SKILLS & DRILLS

SKILLS & DRILLS
For Practical Shooting

BEN STOEGER

Foreword by USPSA Champion Hwansik Kim

Skyhorse Publishing

Copyright © 2018 by Ben Stoeger
Foreword copyright © 2018 by Hwansik Kim
Skyhorse Publishing edition © 2025

Skyhorse Publishing books may be purchased in bulk at special discounts for sales promotion, corporate gifts, fund-raising, or educational purposes. Special editions can also be created to specifications. For details, contact the Special Sales Department, Skyhorse Publishing, 307 West 36th Street, 11th Floor, New York, NY 10018 or info@skyhorsepublishing.com.

Skyhorse® and Skyhorse Publishing® are registered trademarks of Skyhorse Publishing, Inc.®, a Delaware corporation.

Visit our website at www.skyhorsepublishing.com.

Please follow our publisher Tony Lyons on Instagram @tonylyonsisuncertain.

10 9 8 7 6 5 4 3 2 1

Library of Congress Cataloging-in-Publication Data is available on file.

Print ISBN: 978-1-5107-7944-0
eBook ISBN: 978-1-5107-7945-7

Cover design by David Ter-Avanesyan
Cover photograph by Getty Images

Printed in China

CONTENTS

FOREWORD

Growing up in South Korea, I never participated in any sports, and I was never exposed to firearms until I began my two-year mandatory military service. Even then, I only had experience shooting rifles in the army. I did not fire a pistol until I moved to the US when I was 24 years old. It wasn't until two years later that I purchased a pistol and shot my first indoor action shooting event at the age of 26. I fell in love with action shooting competitions, and especially USPSA, almost instantly. At the very first USPSA match I attended, I decided I wanted to be a GM-level shooter and in a couple months, I set my goal to be an IPSC world champion.

I started training as a poor and soon-to-be-married college student living in a small apartment; I needed a way to maximize my training using limited resources to grow quickly in a short amount of time. Through online research, I found the multiple-time national champion, Ben Stoeger, who started training with similar circumstances to mine. I was fascinated by his training methods! At the time, I had never heard about dryfire practice. I started watching his shooting videos and reading his internet posts to figure out what his training was like. I wanted to know how he won a national champion title within six years of shooting.

In my opinion, what makes him a great shooter and a great instructor is that he has the ability to self-coach as well as coach others effectively. Through online research and conversations with some of the world's top shooters, I found many of them have a coach, oftentimes their family. However, Ben was able to be at the top in shooting and teaching despite the fact he never had his own coach. This is very unique, as not all the top shooters have the ability to be a great shooter and a great coach. However, I believe Ben was able to develop his shooting and coaching skills simultaneously. His training materials strongly reflect this strength by demonstrating exactly how to shoot better and how to maintain improvements by self-coaching at the same time. This is a skill that I admire and have sought to gain myself by studying his teaching materials.

When I began pursuing a shooting career, I purchased all of his shooting materials, including *Skills & Drills* (1st edition). As I read the book, I highlighted and color-coded all the important information. The book was always with me when I went to the range. It isn't just a drill book to me, it is something that offers great and practical information. Using the information from Chapters 8 through 10 of the book, I analyze my shooting using my shooting videos and range diary. After that, I come up with a plan that will improve and maintain all aspects of my shooting skills. Once I know what to work on, there are drills from the book that specifically address the shooting skill I want to improve, ranging from fundamental to Hollywood ninja skills. Additionally, it taught me how to make my training sessions more effective by following the guidelines in Chapter 10. What I really like about Ben's materials is that he provides efficient training methods that save time and suit me well. I am not really interested in shortcuts, but I am all about efficient and productive training that will guide me to win matches as soon as possible.

Just by pursuing the par times specified in *Skills & Drills*, I was able to become a master class shooter in USPSA Production division within six months. After I was very convinced that Ben's shooting books actually worked for me, I drove 10 hours to take his *Skills & Drills* class. From the class, I learned how to use his book to my advantage even more than before. Not only that, but I had one of the most important breakthroughs in my shooting career

while taking his class. The breakthrough happened to me when I realized why Ben is one of the best and can win so many matches; it was his discipline in shooting. With this new knowledge, I kept studying Ben's materials and his training methods and applied them to my training to develop everything needed to be the best in shooting. As a result, I was able to win the 2016 USPSA Area 1 Championship in Production Division, with a couple state championship wins, after less than two years of shooting. I was also able to finish 18th overall at the 2016 USPSA Production Nationals and 8th in Production Division at the 2016 IPSC US Nationals. I strongly feel that Ben's instruction played a big part in helping me get to this point.

I believe this book can help anyone from beginners to the best shooters in the world. If anyone wants to train effectively without wasting their ammo and time, this book is a must have.

—Hwansik Kim

WHAT'S NEW IN THIS EDITION?

The first question you may have about a second edition is "Why?" Why do this thing? What needed fixing? If you used the previous version of *Skills & Drills* but got this version in order to keep current, then your initial concern may well be understanding what is different about this version so you can immediately apply those things to your training. The following bit is a brief explanation of what is going on in this book.

First, I decided to reorganize the book. I have retitled many of the sections of drills and have gotten things more in line with how I teach these concepts. For example, I previously had a section for "Field Course Skills," and now I have moved some things out of that section and retitled it "Movement Skills." This new organization better reflects what is going on in the groups of drills, and should make it easier to find things you are looking for.

I have, of course, added in a few new drills. I have done quite a bit of training with other shooters in the last few years. I travel to other continents, occasionally, just to shoot with the top guys and train with them. I have brought the best of these drills and ideas back with me and added them to the book in various places. The new drills are among my favorites and are things that I do frequently. I have deleted a few other drills that I deemed redundant or in some way unnecessary. This was done to keep the number of drills in the book to a manageable size.

The drills themselves have been tweaked in many cases. I have adjusted par times or goals, and/or clarified the commentary on many of the previously existing drills. The diagrams are new. I have also added a place for you to write notes and keep records of your training. This precludes an electronic version of this book, but it does add a bit of function that a few of you were asking for. The bottom line is that things change over time, and this book needs to change with them. I think this second edition of *Skills & Drills* has successfully done that. Longtime users of this material, as well as newcomers, should be satisfied with this new edition of *Skills & Drills*.

WELCOME TO SKILLS & DRILLS

I thought it would be beneficial for me to lay out my approach to training—past, present, and future—to help people understand my journey and the mentality that has led to the creation of this book. I want you to have as much information as possible to assist you in formulating your own plan. Pay special attention to concepts such as goal setting, analysis, and hard work; you will find that these are common themes throughout the book.

Getting Classified

I got started in practical shooting in 2005. I saw competitive shooting on the internet, and I knew it was for me. I was aware the International Defense Pistol Association (IDPA) and USPSA were both practical shooting organizations. At the time, it seemed like IDPA lined up better with what I wanted to do. I wanted to be able to shoot my Beretta 92F, and I didn't want to have to purchase a lot of extra gear. I saw some match footage online, and it seemed to me that USPSA was a "hosefest," and IDPA would be a more balanced test of shooting (for the record, I no longer think this way; it was just what I thought before I knew what I know now).

Because it was winter, and I lived in Wisconsin, I knew I had a couple of months to practice before the start of the shooting season. I had a handful of magazines, and a pistol that I could shoot a respectable group with . . . and

that was it. I purchased a holster, some mag pouches, and a timer, and started doing dryfire. At that point in my life, I had only fired about a thousand rounds of ammo, and I had never really shot fast, but I was anxious to do it.

I did a bit of research, and determined what was needed to become an IDPA Master. It turned out the first IDPA match of the year was a "classifier" match, so I started training for it. For me, it was a simple matter of dissecting the IDPA Classifier. If you don't know, at that time IDPA used a classifier that is a three-stage, 13-string, 90-round event. With a little bit of "googlefu," I determined how fast I needed to draw, how fast my splits needed to be at any given distance, and how many points I could drop. It was relatively easy to get a really good idea of what was needed to obtain a Master classification.

Since I knew I wanted to eventually be competing in USPSA as well, I also took a look at the classification system for that sport. It was vastly more complex than IDPA, but at the same time there were some patterns in it. If you sample the USPSA Classification System, you will see that many of the classifiers are set at 7 or 10 yards. You will see they tend to be straight forward setups. Although things have changed since 2005, I still think it is fair to say that the USPSA "El Presidente" classifier is reflective of the sorts of skills you need to master to be competitive in USPSA.

Interestingly, a version of the "El Presidente" is also included in the IDPA Classifier.

I liked the essence of the classification system for both sports, and I wanted to figure out how to compete at the highest level of each sport. I didn't see the point to being anything other than an IDPA Master (at that time, Master was the highest IDPA classification; Distinguished Master did not exist), and if I was going to shoot USPSA, I didn't see any reason to be anything other than a USPSA Grand Master (GM).

Now, I realize in retrospect how unusual that sort of thinking was, and still is today. I meet a lot of shooters and have a lot of students that just want to move up a class or two. I understand that I am a little bit nuts, but I just figured that if I practiced properly, I would obtain the highest classification in each sport. However, I did not solely want to get a GM card; I wanted to be a GM. There is definitely a difference between simply obtaining a GM classification and being a GM capable of winning a major match. My ultimate goal was not to simply obtain a classification; my goal was, and still is, to win.

After studying the classification systems for each sport, I dug a little deeper. On various internet forums and in books, I found that there were certain levels of skill that were widely considered to be "good." It seemed to me that about a one-second draw at seven yards was the standard. I learned about the "Bill Drill." I learned about lingo like "transitions" and "splits." I learned approximately how fast people needed to be at respective distances to be considered "fast." I also got an

idea of how accurate someone needed to be in order to be considered "accurate."

I also spent a good deal of time reading every single shooting book I could get my hands on. Of course, a few of the great shooters from previous decades had taken the time to write books or make training materials and I found that material enormously helpful. I did the best I could to find unifying themes, things that seemed universal. Things like stressing accuracy and draw speed worked their way into my training from these materials.

This research was the beginning of what I refer to as the "Standard Practice Setup" in the standard exercises section of this book. I didn't invent any of those drills. That information was out there, and it was easy for me to figure out the goal times at 7 or 10 yards. Many people have posted that information online, and for the most part I found it credible. Getting appropriate goal times for drills shot at farther distances is extremely challenging, even to this day.

For example, the following times are what I came up with for my "Standard Practice Setup" found in the standard exercises section:

Distance: 7 yards
1-second draw
2-second "Bill Drill"
2-second "Blake Drill"
0.2-second splits
0.2-second target transitions (with 1 yard between each target)

Distance: 10 yards
5-second "El Presidente"

I want to make it clear that my "Standard Practice Setup" was the exact plan that I used for my initial training program. I did not use any intermediate goal times. I focused on dryfire to help me achieve these goal times. To reach my goals, I developed a simple dryfire plan, but simple does not mean it was easy. I put in endless hours of dedicated dryfire practice before going to the range to fire a single shot. I exhaustively researched shooting techniques from every available resource to make sure I was doing things as best I could.

As soon as the weather got warmer, I started my livefire training. Because of dryfire I was able to consistently execute a one-second draw the first day. The two-second "Bill Drill" took longer. I found it difficult to get my hands to shoot the gun as fast as necessary when firing multiple shots and having recoil control. I chased that time over the course of a few practice sessions before finally being able to do it consistently.

Again, I want to point out that at no time did it enter into my mind that any skill level other than a two-second "Bill Drill" at seven yards was an option. I thought of this strictly as pass/fail. If I got all "A"s in two seconds or less, I passed . . . if not, I failed. I shot a few strings that were literally completely out of control. Conventional instruction would have been that I should slow down and get my hits. I didn't think in those terms. In my mind, slowing down was detrimental to my progression. After a lot of hard work, I was nailing the "Bill Drill" in under two seconds with all "A"s. So, I kept working. I worked at the

"Blake Drill." I worked at the "El Presidente." While still being safe, I shot at speeds where I felt just a little bit "out of control" on each of these drills. After a few weeks of biweekly livefire, I focused on my first match . . . the IDPA Classifier.

I shot the IDPA Classifier in practice a couple of times, and I made sure to familiarize myself with all of the strings. I was able to shoot Master scores consistently in practice, so I figured that I should be able to do that in a match situation. I continued to work the IDPA Classifier in dryfire to make sure I was ready.

At my first IDPA match, I earned the classification of Master. Of course, that surprised some people at the club where I shot, but it didn't surprise me. It seemed to me at the time that it was just a matter of simple math. You have X amount of time to get the pistol out of the holster and shoot the cardboard target in the center. You have X amount of time to fire a follow-up shot. It is as simple as that. As soon as you figure out what time to plug into X, you push yourself in training until X becomes reality.

After a few months of training in this fashion, I started shooting USPSA. I started USPSA with a classifier match, and I did pretty well at it. After my first few matches, I got my initial classification card, and it said GM on it. I was admittedly a little surprised by that. It seemed a bit too easy, but again, it's a matter of simple mathematics. Shoot all "A"s or close "C"s in X time at Y distance.

Shooting Matches

After I obtained my initial classifications in both sports, I started working at being able to do well on actual match stages. For a couple of years, I trained hard. The fundamental problem, and also the main attraction, for practical shooting is that one never really knows what they are going to get. Every stage is different. This means that you have to expand your training in order to get good at a multitude of skills and be able to execute those skills on demand while under match pressure.

I started attending major matches right away. I saw that the classification system didn't completely prepare me for what I encountered at major matches, but at the same time I felt I was well prepared to stand and shoot. However, it seemed I lacked the ability to get from Point A to Point B efficiently.

My theory, initially, was that I would be able to construct a series of drills that included some movement from one position to another. These drills would be set up the same way each time, so I could track my progress on the drills. It seemed perfectly logical to me. Unfortunately, it didn't really work all that well. I didn't see a great deal of change over time on my drill times, at least not much change in the actual time to move from point A to point B. At the same time, I never really felt prepared when I was in a match situation. Things always seemed to be different than the way I practiced them.

To make a long story short, over the course of years, I ended up entirely abandoning the idea of having a repeatable set of movement drills. Instead, I set up mini stages and used them to learn as much as I could that day.

I began to think in terms of scenarios. I worked to get better at coming into a position and whacking a difficult target. I worked to get better at reloading and knocking out an easy target as I moved. I designed mini stages to replicate scenarios that I saw in major matches, and then I worked to improve the required skills.

As I was developing a system for working on my run-and-gun skills, I also cataloged the other things that you see at USPSA matches. Strange positions, unique props, and difficult targets all seemed to pop up from time to time in major matches. After I got burned once, I tried to develop a drill that would help me be better prepared for the next time I encountered that scenario. This was a long process. After every major match, I would carefully analyze the results and look for patterns. Did I have a slow time on a certain type of stage? Did I drop too many points on certain types of targets? The questions were endless. This caused me to constantly refine my approach to how I was training.

It took me about five years until I finally arrived at the complete system that brought me a National Championship. This system included a mix of both live and dryfire drills. I also did quite a large amount of scenario-style training where there was no repeatable setup, and again, this was by design.

During this time, it became my job to teach other people to shoot. I codified my training system in *Skills & Drills* and *Dryfire* in 2013. I brought that system with me all over the United States and used it in classes. The next year, I started bringing that system to other regions all over the world. I taught my training system to as many people as I could, and sometimes even needed to use a translator to convey the information.

My overseas training and match participation further fueled development of my own system. My skills have improved, and so have the classes. This brought me a victory at the European Handgun Championships in 2016.

The current training system that I use shares the broad structure of what I was doing five years ago, but the drills themselves are refined. They are more focused in some areas, and more difficult at times. The goal is still to both be the best I can possibly be, and to make the people around me the best they can be as well. People around me getting better makes me better as well. It is good for everyone and good for the sport. This new edition of *Skills & Drills* is better than ever, and I expect the shooters that apply it to be better than ever as well.

I Have Included the Following Topics:

First, I want to challenge you to examine your own training. Are you effective or are you not?

I then want to examine some different approaches to training. There are many schools of thought on this, and I want to address them.

Next, I want to show you how to practice effectively. I want to give you good tips to cut down the amount of time it takes you on the range, and I want to reduce the round count while you are there.

I want to give you some drills to shoot, and the tools to self-diagnose problems during the drills, so you can actually get better.

I want to show you how to master the USPSA classification system. I don't want you to get a GM card, I want you to become a GM.

I will show you how to meaningfully design practice stages.

Finally, I want to give you the methods to evaluate whether or not you are improving.

I have organized the book like this:
Chapter 1: You Are Doing It Wrong
Chapter 2: How to Use This Book
Chapter 3: Marksmanship Drills
Chapter 4: Transition Drills
Chapter 5: Standard Exercises
Chapter 6: Movement Skills
Chapter 7: Other Skills
Chapter 8: Designing Practice Stages
Chapter 9: Designing Your Training Plan
Chapter 10: Documentation
Chapter 11: Efficient Practice Sessions
Chapter 12: Odds and Ends

Essentially, I am going to outline a training plan. If you actually undertake this plan, I can promise that you will make important gains in your skill level. There are (obviously) many different training plans available to you. This is the plan for the common man. If you are a regular Joe, of regular means, then this is the book for you, especially.

Before We Get Started

This section is designed to lay the foundation for the rest of the material in this book, but first I want to challenge you to examine your own training. Is your current training program effective or not?

I am going to be making some claims about how effective proper training can be. Since the whole point of this book is to make you better at livefire practice with your competition gun, I will not spend a whole lot of time talking about other things.

This book does not specifically address the mental, physical, and technical preparation of a competition shooter. One must understand, however, that those variables are very important for any shooter to reach their full potential.

Prior to implementing the training system outlined in this book, you should already be doing regular dryfire. It has been said by people far smarter than me that if you aren't doing dryfire every day, you aren't training. I think that is very sound advice for the vast majority of people. That being said, I know that there are some top-tier shooters out there that do little to no dryfire training. It is likely unrealistic, however, for you to shoot anywhere near the amount of livefire rounds that they shoot. The bottom line is that dryfire is an extremely important piece of this whole process, and you can use any of the available dryfire training manuals that you want. Obviously, I think my dryfire manual is the best, but you can get better using any of the top manuals available today.

Whichever dryfire program you choose, you should ensure the program gets you to a level where:

1. When you draw the gun from the holster, you get the same grip every time. You can't work with an inconsistent grip in livefire; it just isn't going to do the job.

2. You need to be able to look at any given spot, then draw the pistol and aim at that spot while having the sights show up in near perfect alignment. This is variously referred to as "index," "natural point of aim," or other variation of that. This is a very important skill to possess. You simply must be able to "drive" the gun to where you want it on a subconscious level.

3. As a logical progression of drawing the pistol with the sights aligned, you must be able to look from spot to spot and have your sights show up in alignment on that spot.

4. All gun handling skills, such as drawing and reloading, must be done smoothly and efficiently.

5. You must be able to pull the trigger straight to the rear without disturbing the sight alignment.

Absolutely everything on that list can be developed in dryfire without the use of any live ammunition. Of course, you should go shoot live ammunition occasionally to confirm that you can actually do these things, but the actual training and development can be done without leaving your house.

Furthermore, it needs to be understood that if you wish to change any of your techniques, then you do so during your dryfire training. For example, if during your livefire practice sessions you don't like the way you are gripping your gun, then you take that information to dryfire and make the changes there.

Some researchers and scientists say that it takes anywhere from 3,000 to 10,000 repetitions to learn a new skill. They throw around buzzwords like *neural pathway myelination*. Honestly, I don't know much about the science behind the process, but what I can tell you, through personal experience, is that it is far more efficient to consciously train gun handling skills in dryfire to make that specific skill subconscious. This process may take as little as a week, or with some skills, it has taken me several weeks of dedicated dryfire to make that skill subconscious. Your livefire training will be much more productive if you go to the range with your gun handling skills already programmed so you can execute them subconsciously.

If it sounds like I am telling you that you need to spend a great deal of time doing dryfire, I am. I personally do the vast majority of my training repetitions in dryfire at home. To get the most out of this book, you should consider taking the same approach.

If your goal is to compete at the highest levels of the sport, you must be committed to one shooting setup. It is counterproductive to switch guns, gear, or divisions all the time. Sure, it may be fun, but it isn't helpful for your training. The top pros in the sport are able to do this, but they already own the gear, and they have already developed the skills required to switch from one setup to the other. It is different for a new shooter coming up in the sport. You probably don't have access to the amount of money or time required to be figuring out new stuff every other match.

Again, it is best to pick one set of gear and work with it. It requires some real experience to be able to go from gun to gun without a hiccup.

It is also best if you have your ammunition situation figured out. You don't want to be constantly monkeying around with different loads. Find a load that works properly, and then don't mess with it. Again, as you get some experience and get trained up, screwing around with your reloads isn't a big deal, but you don't want it to consume your range time at first. Just get some stuff that chronographs OK and groups well, and don't worry about it. If, after you start doing some productive training, you want to make a change, then make a change and don't worry about it. Think about it like this, every round you fire over a chronograph is one less round you have to use to actually get better.

What I am getting at here is that if you want the maximum benefit from this book, you should dryfire, settle on a set of gear and a supply of ammo, and then commit yourself to getting better with what you have.

In this book, I will examine some different approaches to training. There are many schools of thought on shooting, and I will address several of them. I will show you how to practice efficiently and effectively by providing you with some tips to cut down the amount of time it takes you on the range and have a more effective training session while reducing your round count. I will give you some drills to shoot, and the tools to diagnose your training and performance when shooting those drills. I will show you how to master the USPSA classification system. I will show you how to design meaningful practice stages. I'm going to outline a training plan for you, and if you dedicate yourself to this plan, I can promise you that you will make significant gains in your skill level.

In summary, **I don't want you to just get a GM card; I want you to become a GM.**

There is one important disclaimer that I want to put forward early on. This information was all developed for Production guns. I believe that the drills and the information will work for any division, but just understand where it is coming from. Any iron sighted shooter should get a lot out of this. If you use an Open gun, I have included information to assist you, but understand that the goal times are going to be a bit too slow.

Chapter 1
YOU ARE DOING IT WRONG

If you are bothering to read this book, then it is likely that you are already on some sort of a training program. This may not be a formalized plan. It may be that you go to the range every Friday and practice with 200 rounds at a time, and then shoot a club match every other week. When I am working with students in a class setting, I find it common to talk to people who shoot roughly 10,000 rounds a year. Some people I work with shoot even more, and some have been doing so for years. If this reminds you of yourself, then read carefully.

You are doing it wrong.

If you have been shooting USPSA regularly for a couple years, then you have no business being in C class.

If you have been shooting for a few years and practice regularly (something like 10,000 rounds a year or more), then there is absolutely no reason for you to be stuck in B class.

If you have been at this for years, are committed to a serious practice schedule, train for major matches, and shoot regularly, you simply shouldn't be stuck in A class.

You are all doing it wrong!

It is time to take a hard look at your own practice methods. When you are at the range, what are you trying to accomplish? Do you have vague and indistinct goals? Do you go out to "work on your accuracy" or "work on your speed?"

It is time to think about your training mindset. Shooting isn't like weightlifting. You don't get better just by doing "reps." Sure, you need repetition in order to improve, but shooting is about more than that. This is a "thinking" game. You need to invest actual mental energy in your training. You need to be involved and engaged in your training. You need to pay attention. Going through the motions will not get you where you want to go.

If you think you are one trick or one little technical change away from greatness, you are kidding yourself. There are no magic pills. There is no snake oil. There are no secrets. There is only training and learning.

Once you accept that you are doing it wrong, then maybe you can start doing it right . . . or at least a little better. I am here to help.

Training Paradigms

I think it would be a helpful exercise to identify a few of the more common training paradigms that I have seen. By "training paradigm," I mean a framework for your training. Everyone does things a little bit differently, and I want you to think about what paradigm you fit into best. Nobody likes to be pigeonholed, but you should take a minute and consider what paradigm you fit into. Then, take another minute and think about where you would like to fit into.

No Real Practice

It is very common to see people in the training paradigm in which they don't really do too much of anything. They show up to club matches or the occasional major match and really don't have very high expectations in terms of results.

These shooters may put themselves in the "I just do this for fun" category. They may not know how to practice. They may not have range access. The reasons for not practicing are virtually endless.

If you find yourself in this category of shooter, then I am a bit surprised you are even reading this book. If you are interested in improvement and want to do better, the bottom line is that you absolutely *can* get better at shooting. You may be thinking that you don't have the time for it. You may think you don't have the money. The fact is, with just a few minutes a day, and maybe 30 bucks a week in practice ammo, you can make huge strides. Your practice should be carefully structured in order to get the most bang for your buck, but certainly you shouldn't let life get in the way of better shooting if that is your goal. Don't be this person.

Used to be Good, Quit Practicing

There are many shooters that used to be hardcore about their training. Maybe they worked hard for a few years and climbed the ranks. Maybe they had a bit of talent and drive and it took them to Master or GM class.

I have met enough of these people to know that the bottom line is that for some reason they lose that spark. They lose the drive that new shooters have. Usually, this is the result of reaching a plateau. Improvement comes so fast and easily in the beginning of your shooting career that when the improvement seemingly stops, it can be extremely demoralizing. If you are a Master class shooter right now, it could take you six months or a year of dedicated training for you to start noticing improvement.

If anything, this is a question of motivation. If you have hit a plateau, and then you give up on training, you can get the spark back. Plenty of people find the spark again when they change divisions or remember how much fun shooting can be. However, without some motivation, you aren't going to get anywhere.

Disorganized

It has become a pop culture phenomenon to insert the word *squirrely* into a sentence to indicate that you should be prescribed Ritalin or something. Does your training require organization? Do you have specific goals? Do you feel like you chase every "shiny thing" you see?

If you are one of the people that goes out and shoots, but doesn't really know what to practice, you may well fall into the "disorganized" category. Disorganized shooters are people that just go out and do their thing. There isn't much of a rhyme, reason, or plan to any of it. Don't be this person.

Dryfire a Lot, Livefire a Little

Most credible trainers recommend a good mix of livefire and dryfire. In prior works, I have recommended a mix of five dryfire trigger pulls for every one livefire pull. I think, generally speaking that makes sense. That works out to doing a bit of dryfire every day and doing a couple days of livefire every week. Of course, not everyone can do that mix. Some people can get to the range about once a week. Some people can't go anywhere near that much.

When you aren't doing livefire on a regular basis, it becomes difficult to progress. It is helpful to feel the way the gun recoils. It is good to see the sights move on the target. It is important to have to drive the sights back to the target. Without these things happening, your training is missing that "reality check" you get from livefire.

I personally experience this during the winter months when I dryfire regularly, but do not livefire. This usually lasts four or five months. I usually get better during that time at the gun handling tasks like drawing and reloading and so on. However, I need to virtually relearn the feel of shooting a gun. The way the gun moves in recoil, the way the trigger operates, and the way the sights track are all virtually foreign after not experiencing it for a few months.

In any event, if your training is all dryfire and very little livefire, don't despair. You can make huge strides that way. You may not be able to get to the pinnacle of the sport without doing livefire, but you can go pretty far.

Sporadic

The sporadic trainer is the person that likes shooting and practices but does so on a very irregular basis. This person may dryfire every day for a few weeks, and then not touch their gun for two months. You never really know what that person is going to do.

Sporadic training obviously isn't a terribly effective way to go about your business. For a training plan to work, you need to stick to the plan. You can't take a week off here or a month off there. When I get into a training flow, I am working at it, learning, and making gains. There isn't any time to slow down.

Sporadic training essentially slows your development, and in my opinion, may well cap your skills at a much lower level than you could otherwise achieve. Don't be this person.

All livefire

There is a relatively small contingent of shooters that falls into this category. These are shooters that have the resources for copious amounts of livefire training, something like three to five times a week, and may well neglect doing any dryfire. This is a huge mistake.

There are many skills that are trained more effectively in dryfire. Just because you are able to livefire until you are up to your ankles in brass doesn't mean that it is the best idea. It is easier to do more repetitions in dryfire. You don't need to paste targets or fill mags, and you can simply focus on training a specific set of skills. Things such as drawing and reloading are more efficient to train without using ammunition.

In the unlikely event that you do an absurd amount of livefire and aren't seeing results from it; the cause could well be that you are neglecting your dryfire. I have met more than one C class shooter that does dedicated livefire training, but no dryfire. Don't be this person.

Worker Bee

If you measure the quality of your training by the quantity, then you are a worker bee. It may sound absolutely crazy to need to point this out, but it is true.

I often get questions from people where they want to know "how many reps" of this drill they should do, or "how many rounds" of that drill they should shoot. The idea of training is to learn and to break through new barriers. How many rounds you shoot or how much time you spend on the range isn't relevant. Of course, being willing to work hard is a great asset, but it won't seal the deal for you.

I have even spoken with a few shooters that think they will win matches because they are willing to "work harder" than everyone else. If another competitor shoots 20,000 rounds a year, then they think they just need to shoot 25,000 rounds a year to beat them. If the best guy at their club does 15 minutes a day of dryfire, then they think they just need to do 20 minutes a day to beat him.

The fact is, it doesn't work like this. There isn't any doubt that practice is closely correlated with skill level, but you can get to where you want to go by applying brain power along with elbow grease.

Also, I should point out that "worker bees" tend to burn out. Since they think working hard is the name of the game to do well, they eventually decide it isn't worth the work. Don't be this person.

Gear Fiend

Some shooters are just never satisfied. I think that is a good quality. A bit of dissatisfaction breeds some ingenuity. Constantly looking for a better way or a better method is great. It makes you better. Constantly looking for a better tool is much the same way.

Everyone knows shooters like this. They are constantly tinkering with guns. They are constantly trying new reloads. They are never happy with how their trigger is set up.

Obviously, this sort of thing can be taken too far. If you spend the start of nearly every practice session testing your new reloads out, then you are wasting a great deal of time and ammo. Once you have a load that is doing the job, you don't need to mess around with it.

Gear fiends tend to attribute a lot of importance to the specifics of the gun they are using and the way it is set up. A very important part of the game is gear, but at the end of the day, the point of training is to develop your skills. You should never forget that. Don't be this person.

Balanced Approach

Obviously, all of the above approaches are flawed in some way. The key to being effective and efficient with your training is to bring some sort of balance to your approach. You need the appropriate amount of dryfire, livefire, gear tinkering, and so on in order to maximize your training benefit. You need to carefully consider what is going to get you to your goals. This requires you to think!

It is difficult for many people to determine where to draw the line between doing the right thing and being counterproductive. If you need to go spend part of a practice session to get some load data, then fine. If you are constantly tinkering with your loads and are spending time testing ammo in every practice session, then you are tinkering around too much and need to stop.

It is essential to carefully and honestly evaluate yourself. You can go far in USPSA without doing a lot in the way of focused training. Some people may make GM with sporadic and unfocused training, but eventually you will need to take the time to systematically improve your approach if you want to compete to win major matches. Many people decide at some point to "work harder," when what needs to happen is they need to change what they are doing. Doing more of the wrong thing, or the suboptimal thing, is not the most efficient way for one to train, and it will likely not be effective in the long term.

Training Myths

I already spent some time addressing the falsehood that you have to shoot an exorbitant amount of ammo every year in order to improve. There are many schools of thought about pistol training floating around out there, and many of them are wrong. The purpose of this section is not to be demeaning about other techniques. My purpose is to be honest and share my personal experiences with you. Because there is so much "bad" advice out there, I feel that I need to "come out swinging" against some of these myths. I think they are counterproductive ideas. These are the sorts of ideas that hold people back. I can't empirically disprove them, but I can tell you that during my own training and interaction with others, both as a shooter and instructor,

I have come to hold some firm positions on how best to train.

Do "Perfect Reps"

I think it is fair to say the idea that you need to make every repetition of your training "perfect" in order to advance is totally false.

I advise people regularly to push themselves to the point of failure. Work until you find what you can't do, and then learn to do that thing. If you want to get better, you have to challenge yourself.

Many people suggest that if you do reps improperly or make mistakes, then you are ingraining bad habits. This is true to some extent, but you shouldn't be afraid to make mistakes. When you consistently do repetitions the wrong way, you will train yourself wrong; there is no doubt about this fact. However, when you find your point of failure and then use it as a learning point, you are going to get better.

The bottom line is, if you want to learn how to shoot quickly, you are going to shoot a *lot* of misses. There simply is no way around it. Don't be afraid; learn and grow as you go.

Pushing for Personal Bests is Pointless

Some people have a problem with the idea of pushing on drills to sct a personal best. People may think that this builds bad habits or gives you an unrealistic idea of your own abilities. Taken to the extreme, I suppose going all out on every single drill may not be productive. Occasionally going all out and trying to push as hard as possible, however, is a great experience and opportunity to learn. This process has allowed me to break through barriers that had been holding me back. You can see new things, shatter expectations, and find that your limits aren't where you thought they were. You will learn what you are actually capable of accomplishing.

Setting a new record on your favorite drill is more than just a set of numbers for your logbook. This can be the motivation that you need, and proof of progress. Pushing for personal bests has fueled my fire to want to continue to get better.

Don't do it every day, but do it. Enjoy it. Learn from it.

Slow is Smooth, Smooth is Fast

One of the least productive axioms in shooting sports is the idea that smooth is fast . . . it *isn't*. As a matter of fact, sometimes the best shooters look strange because they move so fast and explosively. Of course, some of them have the ability to be very fast and also look really smooth, while other top shooters don't look very smooth, but they are still very consistent and fast.

"Slow is smooth, smooth is fast" is the type of advice that makes a good deal of sense when you have literally zero skill, but after a while it wears out its welcome.

You should strive to be smooth when you are first learning a skill, or when you are tweaking an existing skill. For example, if you consciously need to think your way through your draw, then you should focus on being smooth. Once you get it down, speed won't happen on its own. You need to push. You need to work for it.

Work on Accuracy, Speed Will Come

It is common advice to work hard on accuracy with the thought being that eventually you will get faster with some amount of repetition. This isn't the case.

I have known many people that have done a substantial amount of training without any sort of time pressure. They just go out and work on hitting the target in the center every time. Guess what? They don't get faster. As a matter of fact, when they are forced to go fast, like in a match, they usually tank it pretty badly. They just aren't used to the time pressure. It wrecks their fundamentals.

If you want to be fast *and* accurate, then you need to train with a time element. This stuff isn't going to happen on its own; you need to work for it.

Livefire Is Better than Dryfire

I think many people are of the opinion that shooting live rounds is somehow better than doing dryfire. I don't think that is a true statement. We compete with live ammunition, and our actual performance is measured using real bullets, but the majority of your training program will actually be in dryfire (at least if you are following my advice it will be).

It is critical that you don't approach your dryfire training as a less meaningful part of the process. It isn't! Pay full attention during your dryfire and get the most out of it that you possibly can.

Dryfire isn't better and it isn't worse. It isn't less valuable. It has a time and a place. You need to do both livefire *and* dryfire. This isn't optional.

If I Can Shoot Groups, I Am Accurate

It is very often the case that I will meet people that do the majority of their training at high speed on close-range targets. USPSA is mostly about speed, they reason, so the practice needs to reflect that. These people are cognizant of the occasional long target or tight shot, so they know they need to train for those as well. They believe the solution is group shooting.

Unfortunately, this is not terribly effective training. Time pressure adds a whole new element to the longer shots so the shooter will often fall flat on those targets. This is a confusing situation for them. They are able to make hard shots with nearly 100 percent success during practice, but during a match everything falls apart.

Of course, the missing element is the pressure of time. Just because you can make shots slowly doesn't mean you can make them fast. Throwing recoil control and match pressure into the equation doesn't usually equal success. The point of the game is to be able to make tight shots at speed. Nothing less will do.

If I Just Get X Figured Out, I Will Shoot Like a Boss

If you think you are one trick or technique away from greatness, you probably aren't. The fact is that good shooting is the product of good training over a long period of time. After coming into the sport of USPSA, an extremely talented and dedicated person can make it to "super squad" level in something like four to six years. There are certainly exceptions to

that, but most of the top tier shooters I talk to develop somewhere along that timeline.

That is, four to six years of hard training to reach the upper levels of the sport. If that doesn't sound like a long time to you; think again. We are talking about the entire length of time that you were in high school as a bare minimum for reaching the top of the sport. That is a long time to stay motivated and train hard.

If your goals aren't as lofty as being a top 16 GM, then you are still likely looking at a long-time commitment. Even some more pedestrian accomplishments will require months of solid effort to achieve. If you are looking to nail that two-second "Bill Drill" or five-second "El Presidente," then prepare to work for it. There isn't some trick that is going to take you across the finish line.

I Shoot Well, I Just Need to Work on My Stage Skills

On a regular basis, I hear people talk about how they can shoot just as well as anyone, and they just need to work on movement technique, stage planning, or some other aspect of shooting stages.

The reality is that these people are kidding themselves. The best shooters in the game are there because they are the best at shooting. They are the fastest and the most accurate. If you can accept that, it is really going to help drive your training in a positive direction. If you don't accept that, it is going to hinder your advancement. It is that simple.

Chapter 2
HOW TO USE THIS BOOK

In order to get the most out of this book, you should make sure you read all of the organizing material and the core concepts before you start getting into the drills. The drills are located primarily in the middle sections and are divided up by the different skills that they emphasize.

You need to understand training myths, how to set goals, and what you are trying to accomplish in a broader sense before you can maximize your potential.

In short, please do not flip to a drill that looks cool, then go out and start banging away on it. I want you to do some reflection, understand the important concepts that make that a cool drill, and set some goals.

Finally, do not hesitate to alter the drills or add to the drills to make them your own. There is a large degree of creativity required in order to make the ideas in this book useful and relevant. It is counterproductive to slavishly adhere to every word as it is written. If you understand the ideas in this book, consider them carefully, and put in the trigger time, then you should pretty much be able to write your own training book.

Training Blocks

For the past couple of years, I have found it very effective to organize my livefire training into five broad training blocks: marksmanship drills, transition drills, standard exercises, movement skills, and other skills.

A typical livefire practice session is comprised of shooting between two to four scenarios consisting of drills designed to focus on elements of the aforementioned training blocks.

An efficient training session involves very minimal shifting of the range setup. Generally speaking, I design scenarios that are comprised of multiple drills, and those drills are focused on one or more of the training blocks. This allows me to isolate specific skills and analyze my performance easily.

Everyone reading this book has probably heard of some famous drills, and has likely shot some of them. However, it is not the drill that is important, it is the application of the drill and how the drill is shot that is important. A properly designed drill is used to achieve a *specific* purpose. Drills can be used for purposes such as measuring your current skill level, improving your skills, and testing your training progression. You could have a less measurable goal like improving your comfort level with a particular skillset. The utility of properly designed and executed drills is limitless.

I have dedicated entire chapters of this book to address each of the training blocks in detail. The following sections are brief summaries of each training block.

Marksmanship Drills

This skill category involves learning to make difficult shots at speed. Many shooters think that since they can shoot an "acceptable" group size at any given distance, then they must be "accurate enough." Personally, I don't train that way, I am always looking to improve my accuracy at speed. In my world, there is no such thing as accurate enough or good enough. This is why I devote so much training time to making tough shots under time pressure.

Transition Drills

Aside from gun manipulations like drawing and reloading, the thing holding back shooters in terms of raw speed is usually going to be target transitions. This is the time it takes to get from one target to the next target. This is an important enough skillset that I give it its own section for this edition of *Skills & Drills*. This needs to be trained on in livefire (not just dryfire), because you really need feedback from the target score to know whether you are making common errors, like pulling off the target too early.

Standard Exercises

The standard exercises are the things that are going to get you good scores on classifiers. This is where we push the times on our draws, reloads, splits, and transitions. It is obviously a cool thing to be able to do well on classifier stages, but it is also the drills in this category that bring your overall game to the next level by developing your "stand and shoot" skills. All of these drills are repeatable, and they give you a good sense of how you can get faster and better.

Movement Skills

In this section, I break down the skills required to do well in a typical USPSA match. These are the movement skills to get into and out of position quickly and efficiently. This is the stuff that helps you drop seconds off your stage times.

Other Skills

I work on highly technical elements such as moving targets and tight leans in this block of training. I like to work on these elements by themselves, so that I can really see the effect that fractions of time (a quarter second here and a half second there) have on your hit factors for these drills.

"Other skills" is an oddball category. Some stages have you do strange things like load the gun when it is laying empty on a table, or hold a rope with your strong hand and shoot weak hand only. The possibilities are virtually endless. It is true that bigger stages often contain some of these oddball things; however, I like to work on them in isolation. I don't want a lot of other elements to think about, I just want to focus on the stuff I am actually working on.

Concepts to Understand

I would like to take this opportunity to ensure that we are on the same page when we discuss some concepts that are sometimes misunderstood. I want it to be clear when I discuss these concepts later in the book.

Drill Format

The drills in this book are formatted in a way that you should find familiar if you have shot a USPSA style match. There are setup diagrams, start positions, and a stage procedure for each drill described in appropriate detail. Also, I have provided notes as to what the point of shooting that drill is. It helps if you have a firm understanding of handgun technique before you undertake these drills.

For the fundamental marksmanship drills and standard exercises, I provided reasonable goal times. By "reasonable," I mean a time that I feel is achievable with regularity for the average shooter that practices regularly and is properly motivated. The times are designed to push you to Master or Grand Master class in the iron-sighted divisions. Open shooters will need to be just a hair faster. For the more complicated skills, I have provided you with an idea of what your goal should be, but having a specific goal time isn't possible with the more complicated skills.

In any event, these drills are tools. Feel free to modify them. Be creative with them. Use them to get better!

Variable Setups/Repeatable Setups

The drills in this book essentially come in two flavors. Some of them are set up a specific way, and you should set them up that way every time. I have set forth very specific goal times for these drills. These goal times are meaningful. If you want to have the benefit of having that time to reach for, you need to set up the drill exactly as I have it written down. If you choose to set up a drill differently, then

of course that is totally fine, too. However, you must disregard the goal time that I have provided and come up with your own. Also, if you modify a drill, it makes sense to keep that modification in the drill for the duration of the time you use it.

Other drills in this book require that you use a "variable" setup. These are drills where you set up a scenario in order to work on one or more specific elements of your shooting. You do not need to set these drills up the same way every time. As a matter of fact, I don't think you should. These drills are used to help learn technique and learn the sport. You don't need to push toward a specific goal time on these drills.

Variable setup drills will have a narrowly defined purpose, but you are free to set them up to work with your own range situation.

Here is a brief list of examples of elements that you should change in variable setup drills:

- Number of targets
- Target type (steel/paper/partial/mini)
- Target engagement order
- Direction of travel (on movement drills)
- Distance of travel
- Size of props (table height, etc.)

In short, virtually everything is subject to change on these drills. The only limitation is your own imagination. The key thing is that you create the essential scenario called for by the drill, and then work on it. If you are working on shooting on the move, then it matters very much that you create a scenario where you do just that. However, you should adjust all the other elements to make sure you become well rounded. You don't always shoot on the move while you go from right to left. You should do it front to back, back to front, left to right, diagonally, etc. Change all the applicable elements in this fashion as you work on variable setup drills.

Pacing vs. Technique

You should be sure to distinguish between changing techniques and simply "going faster."

Of course, going fast is an important consideration, but when you are trying to learn the game, you need to figure out what sort of aiming methods produce what sort of points and time in any given situation. For example, shooting close targets with a "target focus" is usually faster than going with a "sight focus." The point is that you are going to have a hard time figuring that stuff out if you aren't in control of your pacing.

At the higher level of the sport, you need to be able to cruise through most stages and reserve making a "push" for only when you deem it appropriate. If you want to learn to be in control of your shooting pace, then learn that control in practice.

I have outlined a few shooting "paces" below.

Just Shooting

Often, I like to "just shoot" a drill or stage. This means that I walk through and prepare to shoot the drill the same as I would a stage at a match. I am trying to shoot the best score I can, but I am not going to go past what I think I am capable of repeatedly doing.

In a sense, when I shoot a drill in this mindset, I simply execute the drill and observe what happens. I am not trying to go all out as fast as I can, nor am I playing it conservative. I simply step to the line and do what I know how to do.

This may seem like a pointless thing to do during your training. You might think that you should always be pushing to do better or always focus on perfect execution. Sometimes, it is helpful to step up to the line and do what you know how to do. No more, no less. In this way, you can check your times on various things, like drawing or reloading, in the context of a drill. During that drill, you don't try to push to manipulate that time one way or the other. You just let your body run its natural pace. This is the ideal way to shoot matches.

Pushing

It is frequently the case during your training that you should push. Pushing is when you run a drill or stage faster than you feel comfortable going. Once you get to the point where you plateau, pushing is one of the most important things you can do to improve.

When you push a run on a stage, you run a higher risk of making mistakes. You may mess up a reload, miss your grip on the gun when you draw, or get misses on targets. This isn't a cause for concern when you are pushing. The whole point of pushing is to go to the point of making a mistake or failing, and then working to fix whatever deficiency caused it. Much of my training is done this way.

I want to take a second to point out that pushing isn't just about going faster. Of course, going faster than you are comfortable is an important tool. You will get a sense of what the next level of speed feels like. You will get an idea of what you need to do to acclimate yourself in terms of getting comfortable with going fast. While all of that is true, it is only half the story.

When you push, try not to think only in terms of going faster. Think in terms of utilizing a technique that will produce a faster time. For example, instead of shooting with a front sight focus at some distance, try shooting with a target focus. That method will produce faster times, but in theory you will drop more points. Selecting a faster aiming method is one way to push the time down on a run. It is important to understand, though, that slinging lead as fast as you can isn't necessarily the best practice method. Training yourself to sling lead faster using some specific technique is a whole different idea.

Let me also point out that being able to perform some task on a consistent basis is a prerequisite for pushing your skills. For example, if you can't consistently nail reloads without having some sort of hiccup, then it doesn't make a great deal of sense to try and go as fast you can and push for a really smoking reload time. Pushing comes after you are able to do that skill consistently, on demand, under the pressure of time.

Play it Safe

In the context of shooting, the opposite of pushing is to "play it safe." People often conceptualize this as "slowing down to get their hits." When you are playing it safe, you are trying to minimize the possibility of a mistake. What I normally do is select an aiming method that is a bit more precise than is required for any given target. Note that this isn't the same thing as just slowing down. When people try to execute the same techniques they always do, but just go slower, they still tend to make mistakes. For example, if you decide to play it safe on a 25-yard target and just go slow to get your hits, you will likely execute the same way you always do and end up with similar points and a slower time. If you instead decide to press the trigger really carefully, you will likely have a slower time, but will have better points.

It is important to occasionally train to have a "safe" run. Sometimes, you want to have the ability to execute the safe run at a match. It is nice to be able to skate through a difficult stage without any issues while your competitors suffer from misses and no-shoot hits.

Breaking it Down

One of the most critical things that can be done during training is to break a big drill down into smaller parts. I am going to get into this process in detail during the standard exercises section. For now, just trust me; it's important.

Whenever you shoot a drill or a series of targets, if you take the time to score, you end up with two numbers—a time and a point total. However, you can get a lot more data by using the review function on your timer and looking at each of the split times. You can also check your draw time, transition times, and split times. Once you have this data, then you can attempt to improve each of those elements during subsequent training. As a result, this will ultimately reduce the total time on the drill. This is a very important process, trust me!

Making Mistakes

Generally speaking, people have the idea that if they screw something up in practice, then they are permanently damaging their shooting. I don't agree with this school of thought. Many mistakes will be made on the road to a good performance. Mistakes are things that you should hate. You need to make the mistake, hate the mistake, and then overcome the mistake.

Mistakes happen. Failure happens. Don't hide from it; attack it head on.

Chapter 3
MARKSMANSHIP DRILLS

This is the section of the book containing the drills that are designed to work your core marksmanship skills.

It is my firm belief that these are the most important skills and drills. Being able to make tight shots at speed is the most critical skill for doing well at high levels of competition. Many shooters (especially Grand Masters) are resistant to improving their marksmanship fundamentals. They think that improvement will come from being craftier at breaking down stages, better gear, or some other means. In truth, the people with the best fundamentals are the ones that tend to do the best, and there just isn't any way around it.

In *Practical Pistol Reloaded* I proposed that grip, trigger control, and the draw are all closely interrelated. Similarly, the drills in this section will have you draw the gun and build your grip from the holster. After that, you execute good trigger control, and make good shots. If you screw up any part of the process, you will have a poor performance on the drill. Missing your grip on the draw or slapping the trigger carelessly will be a big problem on these drills.

As much as shooters want to work on "advanced" things like stage strategy and shooting while moving, they should always remember that they need to constantly work to improve their fundamentals. It is always time well spent to continually improve the "basics."

Group Shooting

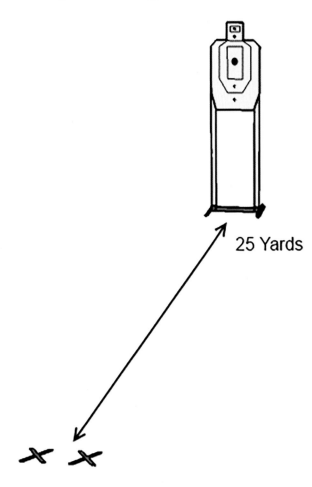

25 Yards

Procedure:

Fire a string of shots into the target. Be as accurate as possible. This drill is *not* timed.

Focus:

Shoot as perfectly as you can. Pay attention to sight alignment and trigger control.

Goal:

The goal with group shooting is to shoot your gun as well as your gun is mechanically capable of shooting. If your gun/ammo combination is capable of three-inch groups at 25 yards, then you want to be able to produce that out of your hands.

Commentary:

Shooting groups is one of those things that you will do early on in your shooting career, and you will never really stop doing it. It may strike you as silly to devote time and energy to a skill that doesn't seem to have that much direct application to USPSA, but there is a lot

Date:	Par Time:	Notes:
	NA	
	NA	
	NA	
	NA	
	NA	
	NA	
	NA	
	NA	
	NA	
	NA	

to be learned here. Working toward mastery of shooting without any time limit will give you the tools to zero your gun in without help from anyone else, to detect problems with your equipment if something isn't working right, and to give you the confidence when you move to high-speed shooting that the gun is capable of hitting exactly where you point it. There can be no substitute for that.

There are a couple of major concerns that I want to point out.

First, being able to shoot tight groups is a different skill than being accurate at speed. When you are pushing to go fast, it tempts you to push down hard on the gun to try to control recoil. Sometimes, people pull the trigger with their whole hand instead of just the trigger finger. During slow fire, people are more tempted to try to discharge the gun at the moment the sights look perfect, and that often results in an errant shot due to rushing the trigger press. The point with all this is that you are dealing with a different set of problems when you are shooting a group vs. shooting under time pressure. Just because you are good at one doesn't mean you will be good at the other.

The second major concern with this exercise is to understand that no time limit means *no time limit*. You should shoot each shot individually. You can lower the gun down to rest between shots. If you start pressing the trigger and you don't like what you are seeing, you can abort the shot and start over. This is a totally different mentality than USPSA shooting, and that is absolutely OK. Do not rush.

The procedure lists that you will fire a "string" of shots into the target and I thought it would be helpful to delve into that a little bit more.

A string of shots could be any number. People commonly shoot 5 shots, 6 shots, or 10 shots, but all of that is arbitrary. One thing that may be helpful is for you to pick some number of shots that you are going to shoot and then stick with it for the rest of your shooting career. Obviously, it is harder to fire 10 perfect shots in a row than it is to fire 2 perfect shots in a row, so the higher the number of shots you fire, the larger the group will tend to be. If you just pick a number that you like and stick with it, you should have some basis for comparison over time or with different types of ammo and so on.

You also have a good deal of targets to choose from. I don't think you should restrict yourself to USPSA/IPSC legal targets for group shooting. Other targets work well too. There are a variety of stick-on targets you could use or paper bullseye targets or some other target. The diagram is shown with a black mark made in the center of the USPSA target. That is also perfectly acceptable.

The reason for using a different target for group shooting is that most people find it much easier to shoot a good group when they have a very definitive aiming point. Some experimentation can be helpful with this. A one-inch square may well be far too small at 25 yards, but an area the size of the "A" zone may be far too big. Your personal preferences will play into it a lot as you experiment with different target arrangements.

I also set the distance on the diagram to 25 yards. This is one of the more popular distances for group shooting, but it isn't your only option. Obviously, you can pick any distance you like. Personally, I have been gravitating toward 50 yards due to using a gun that is far more mechanically accurate than most other Production guns. It all depends on you.

One other concern I should point out is that when you are shooting groups, there are two important considerations. First, you want all the rounds you fire to impact as close to each other as possible . . . obviously. However, you also want the rounds to hit in the center of the target. I would treat these as separate issues. A tight group far from the center of the target could mean there is a problem with the sights, or that you are making the exact same fundamental error every time. It is important to pay close attention and figure it out.

Another thing you should consider is using sandbags or a rest to help you stabilize the gun. I personally avoid this, but other shooters really like it. It is largely a matter of preference. Bagging the gun in will probably give you tighter groups, but I like dealing with the little bit of sight movement you get when you are in a standing position.

The key to good group shooting is accepting that there is some wobble in your sights and trying to discharge the gun without making that wobble any worse. Any sort of flinch, trigger jerk, preignition push, and so on will show up big time during group shooting. You really can never be too good at this skill.

Variations:

Standing and shooting freestyle or sitting at a bench and shooting from a supported position are the standard ways to shoot groups, but they aren't the only ways. You could shoot from around a barricade, shoot one-handed, shoot prone, and so forth. There is no reason not to try shooting groups from different positions.

If you are shooting a DA/SA pistol, you can also try shooting groups with different trigger modes. All single-action, double-action first shot, then single-action, or all double-action shots are all valid ways to shoot groups. Many shooters neglect double-action shooting, but there is no reason to do that.

Practical Accuracy

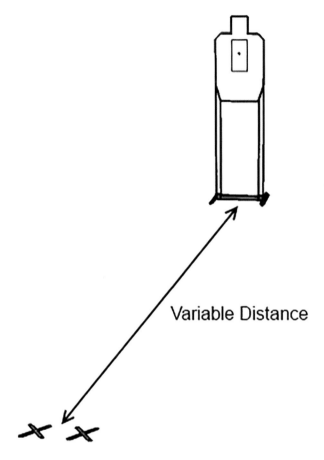

Variable Distance

Setup Notes:

For this drill you need to make the target an "A" zone only. You should paint around the "A" zone using black (hard cover paint). Another option is to cut the "A" zone out of the target and turn it around so you have an "A" zone surrounded by white, creating a no-shoot all the way around the "A" zone.

Procedure:

Pick a distance to shoot from. A good place to start is at 10 yards. At the start signal, engage the target with six rounds. Strive to shoot as tight a group as possible in the center of the target. There is no specific time limit for this drill, but you are required to press the trigger again as soon as your sight returns from recoil and stabilizes in the center of the "A" zone. Shoot six strings from your chosen distance, a total of 36 rounds, then assess the target.

Date:	Par Time:	Notes:
	NA	
	NA	
	NA	
	NA	
	NA	
	NA	
	NA	
	NA	
	NA	
	NA	

Focus:

This drill emphasizes both marksmanship fundamentals and discipline.

Goal:

Shoot six successful strings at your chosen distance. Do not miss the "A" zone once out of those 36 shots. If you are able, move farther away from the target and do another set of strings. If you are able to successfully "pass" this drill at 20 yards, that is adequate for competition.

Commentary:

Before I get into the commentary for this drill, I need to clarify the instructions to make sure that confusion is minimized.

Regarding the time limit: There is no specific time limit for this drill, but that doesn't excuse you from shooting fast. The reason there is no time limit is that I want the drill to work for every level of shooter. It takes you as long as it takes to draw the gun and get a proper grip. You shouldn't try to fix that here. That doesn't mean you aren't concerned at all with speed. When the sights come out of recoil, you should begin to fire the next shot. This is essentially the same thing you ought to be doing at a match. You shoot the speed of your sights; no faster and no slower. If you insist on having some way to measure whether you are going fast enough, I think the range of times is between four seconds and six seconds for average strings. This depends on distance (10 to 25 yards).

Regarding the distances, the usual way I do this drill is to do it at 10 yards, then 15, then 20, and so on. It gets a bit silly at 25

yards just due to the difficulty, but I still do it at that distance . . . and sometimes further. It is OK to start further back than 10 yards if you aren't challenged by that close of a target. That isn't a problem.

The last bit of clarification required here is to the accuracy standard. Do not use the entire "A" zone as your target. You should strive to lay the shots right on top of each other in the center of the "A" zone. The idea here is to attempt to be perfect with every shot, and not to settle for "good enough." This is a strange thing because it is different than normal shooting where you shoot good enough, and just go as fast as you can.

With the clarifications out of the way, I can now move into discussion of the actual drill. As far as my own training goes, this drill is a much more useful variation of group shooting. This is about working on the fundamentals of shooting in the context of shooting at realistic "match pace." Grip, sight picture, and trigger control are the things you should be watching here. You should approach it both from a diagnostic perspective where you try to fix problems, and from an observational perspective where you simply see what is happening. If you detect that you are putting pressure into the trigger a little bit sideways or something like that, then you can implement a fix. You need to pay awfully close attention in order to spot little errors.

Finally, a big part of this drill comes down to discipline. The directions do not call for one good string every now then. They instruct you to shoot string after string after string and have them all be good. This builds the confidence to know that you can make tough shots without having to worry. That mindset will pay off big time at major matches when the pressure is really on.

Variations:

A common variation for me is to shoot this drill one-handed. You don't fundamentally change anything, just go either strong hand only or weak hand only. Obviously, you will need to push back to 25 yards when you are shooting with only one hand to enjoy any serious benefits to your skill level. It is not an easy thing to even do this drill freestyle, so prepare to really hop on the learning curve if you are going weak hand only.

Another thing you can do is to work this drill from an awkward position. Leaning around a barricade is a favorite of mine. You should pay attention to the little points when your position gets awkward. The gun will not behave the same in recoil; it will probably feel quite odd. It is good to learn to shoot through that sensation and still produce good results on target.

Doubles

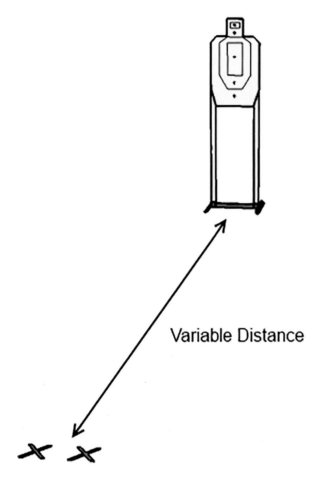

Variable Distance

Procedure:
Start at your desired distance with hands relaxed at sides. At the signal, draw and get a sight picture on the target. When you have your sight picture, fire a pair of shots at your predetermined pace (details below). Stabilize the gun on target again, get a sight picture and then fire another pair at the same pre-determined pace. Repeat this process until you have fired a total of four pairs (eight rounds). Fire six strings at the target for a total of 48 rounds, then assess the target and score it. Work at all distances between 5 and 25 yards.

Focus:
This drill emphasizes marksmanship fundamentals while shooting at a practical pace.

Goal:
To first learn the limits of your skill level regarding potential speed and accuracy, and then to work to improve it. Make sure you

Date:	Par Time:	Notes:
	NA	
	NA	
	NA	
	NA	
	NA	
	NA	
	NA	
	NA	
	NA	
	NA	

aren't pushing follow-up shots down into the target or letting them go over the target. See the guidelines below for specific guidance on split speed and points down.

Guidelines for pace and accuracy:

5 yards	.20 split	95% Alpha
10 yards	.22 split	90% Alpha
15 yards	.25 split	80% Alpha
20 yards	.30 split	70% Alpha
25 yards	.35 split	60% Alpha

Commentary:

This drill requires quite a bit of explanation before I can get into commentary regarding the drill itself.

First, I will call your attention to the "focus" of the drill. The idea here is to work on sight alignment, trigger control, and grip while you shoot at a "practical" pace. So, the pace here is a requirement. You are absolutely required to shoot the split times stipulated by the guidelines. At close range, you will fire pairs into the target essentially as fast as you can pull the trigger. At longer ranges, you will back off the speed a bit.

I should also clarify regarding firing pairs into the targets. The normal engagement sequence on a stage is that you look at the target, drive the gun to the target, and then fire two rounds into the target. On this drill, we are concerned with the actual shooting mechanics and nothing else. I want you to fire multiple pairs in a string, the same as you would in a match, but I want the target transition element removed from the equation. This is the reason you fire four pairs of shots into

the same target rather than four targets. You need to simulate that target transition. The point here is that you should NOT fire eight shots as fast as you can. You should be engaging the target with pairs just like you would in a match.

Another thing that needs to be discussed here is the idea of a "double tap" vs. a "controlled pair." I understand that most shooters want to see their sights for every round they fire. They don't want to be out of control in any sense. The reality of the situation is that in order to be competitive you will not have time to consciously confirm each sight picture on close ranged targets. When shooting this drill you should accept that reality and work with it.

The reason you must shoot in pairs is because it creates some interesting marksmanship challenges, and allows you to deal with them. When people shoot as fast as they can pull the trigger (as they often do in a match), they often push the gun down as they fire the second shot, pull the trigger sideways, pull the trigger with their whole hand, or hold the gun too loose and let it fly all over the place. If you are doing this drill properly, you should at first experience those problems, and then be able to solve them. You are required to shoot quickly, so the usual method of excessively slowing down in order to shoot better points will not work on this drill. That will be a fail.

You should also take note of how many points down are acceptable at longer ranges. Again, this simply is reality in matches. At extended ranges, shooting 60 percent Alpha hits and 40 percent Charlie hits is actually pretty good when you are going match speed. Again, this drill acknowledges those realities. I recommend shooting six strings of eight shots, and then scoring the targets. This will allow you to get a big sample size so that you know how many points you are dropping, and whether or not that meets the standard.

You should also know that you can use the recommended split times to back off in terms of speed. If you shoot 50 percent Alpha hits at 20 yards, but are shooting .22 or .23 splits on average, according to the guidelines it is

acceptable to back off speed a tiny bit if it produces better points on the target. Be aware of that.

From a technique perspective on this drill, you should pay very close attention to your hands. I pay very little mind to sight alignment. That is the easy part. What does matter is feeling a rock-solid grip on the gun, and then feeling my firing hand discharge the gun without pushing it around. If you can master the ability to hold the gun like that, then you will master this drill.

2 at 25

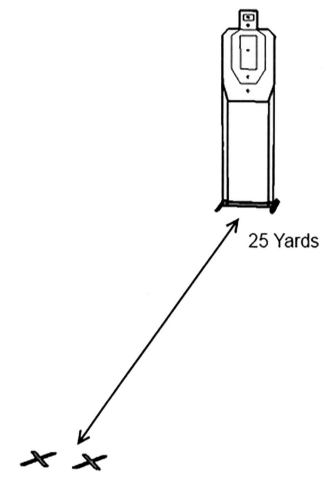

25 Yards

Procedure:

Start with your hands relaxed at sides. At the start signal, draw and engage the target with two rounds.

Focus:

The focus of this drill is to work on basic marksmanship mechanics. The draw, the grip, and trigger control all need to be correct in order to score alphas at speed.

Goal:

Two "A" zone hits in two seconds is a very reasonable and achievable goal.

Commentary:

It is important for those that want to excel at practical shooting to be able to make difficult shots under time pressure. The point of this drill is to get you going down the road to being able to do that.

Let me explain why this drill is set up the way it is.

Date:	Par Time:	Notes:
	NA	
	NA	
	NA	
	NA	
	NA	
	NA	
	NA	
	NA	
	NA	
	NA	

The distance of 25 yards was selected for this drill because to hit an "A" at 25 yards, you need to do pretty much everything right. You need the sights to be lined up more or less perfectly. You need to press the trigger straight back. You need to support all of this with a solid grip.

The reason you are going to fire two shots, instead of one shot, is that it helps to eliminate a luck element and forces you to return the gun down to the target out of recoil. It amps up the difficulty of this drill considerably to need to make two "A" zone hits in rapid succession. The second shot essentially keeps you from drawing the gun out of the holster and getting an "A" more by luck than skill, then thinking that you were successful on the drill.

This drill is simple to shoot, yet difficult to master.

First, the draw is extremely important. You need to snatch the gun from the holster quickly. You can't screw around at all if you want to make the two-second time limit for the drill. For most shooters, the draw time will be 1.3 or 1.4 seconds, leaving the remainder of the time to return the gun out of recoil and make the second shot. This means that you need to draw just as quickly as you would on a close-range target, but then spend a little bit of time (a few tenths of a second) refining your sight picture and working the trigger carefully. A fast and consistent draw is critical.

Next, you need to get the same grip on your pistol every single time. If your grip is off by even a few millimeters, your sights will not come to the target in alignment. You must then either spend a few tenths of a second correcting the sight alignment or fire a poorly aimed shot. Both of those things are bad. Grip consistency is key.

Finally, trigger control is ultimately what is going to make you successful on the drill. You need to develop a careful trigger press for this drill. Ultimately, this is a different sort of trigger control than you would do on a close-range target. If the sights are wobbling slightly, you need to ignore that and just work the trigger straight on back.

25-Yard Bill Drill

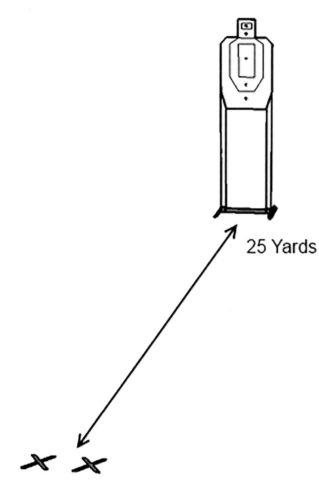

25 Yards

Procedure:
Starting with your hands relaxed at sides, draw and engage the target with six rounds.

Focus:
This drill emphasizes good fundamentals along with staying in control of your shooting pace.

Goal:
All "A" zone hits in four seconds or less is a great goal. Under 3 seconds with "A"s and close "C"s is very impressive.

Commentary:
The classic "Bill Drill" is done at seven yards; I address it later on. For this variation, you move back to the 25-yard line.

Just like the other drills in this section, your marksmanship fundamentals are absolutely paramount. This six-shot drill has some additional elements thrown in.

Date:	Par Time:	Notes:
	NA	
	NA	
	NA	
	NA	
	NA	
	NA	
	NA	
	NA	
	NA	
	NA	

First, there is definitely a "sight tracking" element going on there. Watching your front sight move up in recoil, then using your hand muscles to return the sight, then breaking the next shot is a cycle that you go through time after time in this drill. You need to manage the gun in recoil over the course of every shot. If your hand slips off the grip, or something else happens, then you are going to be in trouble.

There is a pacing issue present in this drill. Many people fire three or four shots and everything looks good. They then start working the trigger faster and breaking the shots a bit quicker. If shots get broken too quickly, then it is common to sling shots over the top of the target because the gun will not be returning out of recoil before the next shot breaks.

A good rule of thumb to keep in mind is that most people have a total time on "Bill Drills" that is about double their draw time. So, for example, if the draw time on the timer reads 1.59 seconds, then usually the total time for the drill will be about 3.2 seconds. If you evaluate your time like this and see a big discrepancy, then you may want to approach the drill differently. For example, if you have a 2.5 second first shot, but a total time in the drill of 3.5 seconds, then you are really running the trigger quickly. If you have widely scattered hits on the target, or misses, you should probably back off your shooting pace. If you are driving lots of "A"s, then you know you have some work to do on your draw.

In terms of scoring, your goal should be to shoot all "A"s, but realistically that is tough to do. Getting all "A"s or close "C"s consistently is pretty good. That will set you up

to sometimes get all "A"s. If you are shooting "D"s or misses, then you have a problem. A "D" hit is basically a lucky miss, and a miss is a miss. You don't want that to happen on this drill. However, as you push on the speed, you will invariably suffer some poor performances. If you miss your grip a little bit, then you may well have three misses out of your six shots. When that happens, just remember the underlying problem was your grip. When you get to matches, you aren't going to push your draw that way, so that if you make a mistake it probably will not be a total disaster.

In terms of scoring, you have a few viable options. You could try only scoring runs that are all "A"s, you could calculate hit factor, or you could work within a par time. Each has its advantages and disadvantages.

If you calculate a hit factor for this drill, you will likely average a higher score by dropping quite a few points. A 25-yard target over the course of a big stage would likely need to be addressed differently than this. On big stages, all the movement and other stuff adds non-shooting time to the stage and drags the hit factor down; it is not so on this drill. Keep that in mind when you start calculating hit factors.

Only "counting" runs that are all "A"s is another option, but it will likely push you a little bit toward the conservative side. In USPSA, it doesn't pay to shoot at a pace that will always net you all "A"s. A few "C"s now and again are acceptable.

This means that working within a reasonable par time is probably the best way to go on this drill. For example, if you can comfortably shoot the drill in about five seconds, then set the par time a bit tighter (like 4.5 seconds). Work within that par time to try to shoot all the "A"s you can with some consistency.

There is so much to be learned from this drill, I feel it is absolutely key to work at it.

Variations:

In addition to the scoring variations that I mentioned previously, you could try this drill strong hand only or weak hand only. Now, 25 yards is a bit of a stretch to shoot only one-handed, but it is certainly an option.

50-Yard Bill Drill

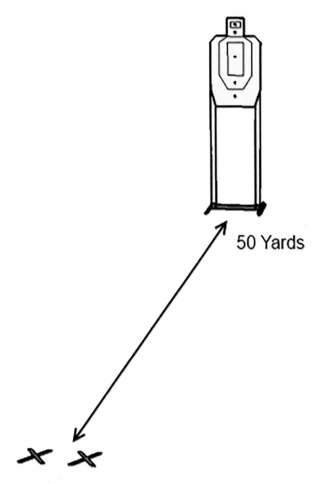

50 Yards

Procedure:
Starting with your hands relaxed at sides, draw and engage the target with six rounds.

Focus:
This drill emphasizes good fundamentals along with staying in control of your shooting pace.

Goal:
All "A" zone hits in six seconds or less is an extremely tough thing to do. Being able to consistently hit the target at 50 yards while shooting with some degree of speed is a rare skill in this sport.

Commentary:
The 50-yard "Bill Drill" is obviously the same sort of idea as the 25-yard "Bill Drill," but it plays out a lot differently due to the *vastly* increased difficulty level.

I think at closer ranges (25 yards and less) you will find that your sights can have a

Date:	Par Time:	Notes:
	NA	
	NA	
	NA	
	NA	
	NA	
	NA	
	NA	
	NA	
	NA	
	NA	

certain degree of motion in them. Your sights never really need to perfectly settle down. You can hit "A"s with rock-solid trigger control. However, at the 50-yard line, everything really does need to be perfect in order for you to hit an "A."

At 50 yards, I like to make sure my sights are perfectly stable, then I start to work the trigger again. After the shot breaks, I return the sights out of recoil, stabilize them, and then break the next shot. The level of stability you need to have in order to do this well is incredible. There are many times when shooting from 50 yards that I would swear everything looked perfect, but when I go downrange I have a miss or something that I didn't see happen from behind the gun.

Many shooters will skip over this drill. They will deem it unnecessary or stupid to shoot at this range. You may well not have a range where you can get this much distance on the targets. However, if you are able to get to a bay large enough to shoot 50 yards, I strongly recommend you try it. You will learn a great deal from this drill, trust me.

One other important thing to point out is that at 50 yards you may well have some equipment limitations. Most Production guns with factory ammo aren't exactly tack drivers at that range. Your gun may well group larger than the "A" zone. This doesn't necessarily make your gun unsuitable for competition, but understand that if your gun doesn't group all that tight to begin with, shooting all "A"s may have an element of luck to it. With my old Beretta, for example, the gun grouped five to six inches at 50 yards. My Witness Elite Stock 2 groups more like three to four inches. It doesn't sound like much, but it makes a big difference during drills.

Variations:

If you are new to long distance shooting, then a six-second par time to fire six shots at 50 yards is a daunting task. It is almost counterproductive to try to produce that time right away. I recommend starting slow fire at 50 yards in order to make sure you can put all your shots on paper with no time limit. You need to know exactly how to align the sights on the target and so forth. If you need to hold a few inches higher up on the target in order to hit the center of it, that is a good thing to know.

After you are able to shoot the target in slow fire, then try working in a time limit. It doesn't have to be very demanding; 10 seconds will go by in a hurry at the 50-yard line, I assure you. As soon as you are able to produce good hits with any given time limit, work the time limit down.

The bottom line is that you will drop a lot of points at 50 yards, and you will be frustrated. Don't give up. Work at it, and you will get better.

The Dots

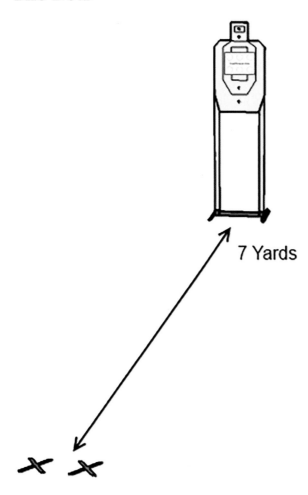

7 Yards

Setup Notes:

This drill requires the use of two-inch diameter dots. I have sheets of them available at www.benstoeger.com. They can be printed off and attached to a USPSA cardboard target. You could also craft a stencil and paint two-inch dots on targets using spray paint. There are a number of solutions available; be creative. The bottom line is that you need a two-inch circle to shoot at.

Procedure:

Starting with your hands relaxed at sides, draw and engage one dot with six rounds. You do not transition between dots; you only engage one. There is a five-second par time for this drill. Give yourself a 0.3-second grace period for overtime shots (anything 5.31 or over will be overtime).

This drill is multiple string. You repeat shooting six rounds into one dot six times, for a total of 36 rounds fired, 6 rounds per dot.

Date:	Par Time:	Notes:
	NA	
	NA	
	NA	
	NA	
	NA	
	NA	
	NA	
	NA	
	NA	
	NA	

This drill is pass/fail. If you get 36 hits, you pass. If you get less than 36 hits, you fail.

Score the dots like you would a USPSA target. That means a hit where the bullet radius touches the outside line of the dot counts as a hit (the bullet doesn't need to hit entirely within the dot).

Focus:

This drill tests skills similar enough to a 25-yard "Bill Drill," but there is an added element of consistency required. The goal here isn't just to shoot hits on the dots; it is to never shoot misses. To successfully go 36/36 on this drill requires you to be something of a machine.

Goal:

Once again, 36/36.

Commentary:

Frank Garcia's dots or "The Dots," as it has come to be known, is a fantastic drill. It is a phenomenally difficult shooting challenge, and a great way to learn.

When you set up a two-inch dot at seven yards, it probably will not look like a very challenging target. The key thing to remember is that your goal isn't to simply hit that dot; it is to become proficient enough that you rarely miss it. This skill level will require a solid fundamental grounding and a good deal of discipline.

I have been using these two-inch dots as targets in training classes for long enough to see that the skills you learn here will be called upon on a lot of USPSA stages. You need to be able to flip on that high level of accuracy and trigger control just like flipping a light switch, and this is the way to develop it.

If you compare that two-inch circle at 7 yards to something like a 25-yard steel plate, I think you will find they appear to be similar difficulty. However, by working on the closer dots, you save yourself a lot of resetting time on falling steel. You also take away the audible feedback element that you get from steel. I prefer these dots to steel targets for that reason.

Another interesting element to this drill is the focal shift that can occur. When you are trying for a really sharp sight focus, it can be difficult to maintain it when you are standing only about 20 feet from the target. Most people print out their dots on white sheets of paper, and that white can really suck your eye to the paper (away from the sights). I frequently find my eyes being pulled forward to the target. You can see the holes appearing in the paper and that can make things even worse. It is a battle to maintain focus on your sights during this drill.

One final element is that there will be some pressure on this one. Maybe when you start with it, you will expect to fail, so there will not be much pressure. However, as you develop, you may occasionally shoot a successful string. After a while you may think that you could possibly go 36/36. Believe me, there is tangible pressure when you are on the range actually doing the drill. If you get three or four strings in a row successfully, you may well feel some intense anxiety as you get to the point of possibly going 36/36. Overcoming that pressure and finishing the drill successfully is a real achievement.

Variations:

Of course, seven yards is going to be tough to start off with. I recommend starting closer. Firing six rounds in five seconds from the five-yard line is going to challenge most any USPSA shooter. Newer shooters may want to start at three yards. I recommend leaving the time limit the same and adjusting the distance to make it easier if necessary. If you still can't do it, try cutting down the number of rounds.

Work up to six rounds in five seconds at seven yards slowly.

If you are using an Open gun, or are extremely accomplished with iron sights, you may want to push back to 10 yards and work the drill at that distance.

It may be tempting to remove the time limit from this drill and just work on hitting the dot with no time limit. That pretty much turns this drill into group shooting. Group shooting is fine, but the speed element to this drill is what makes it challenging. Work with a time limit.

Tight Shots

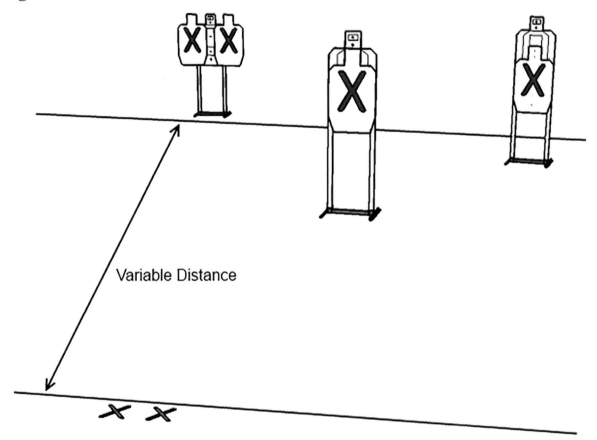

Variable Distance

Date:	Par Time:	Notes:
	NA	
	NA	
	NA	
	NA	
	NA	
	NA	
	NA	
	NA	
	NA	
	NA	

Variable Setup:

This is a "variable setup" drill. I outline a concept for a drill, and then you can construct it based on your own situation. Do not attempt to recreate the diagram. You should create the scenario outlined in the setup notes. The "How to Use This Book" section has more information on variable setups.

Setup Notes:

This drill will be three partial targets set at a distance that will challenge you. The challenge will be for you to shoot at your regular match pace and score no misses, nor no-shoot penalties. If you set it up so that you can't ever get through the drill without clipping a no-shoot, make it a bit easier. The opposite is true as well, if you don't feel challenged, then you need to either move back away from the targets or tighten up the positioning of the no-shoots.

For reference, I usually shoot this sort of drill at between 30 and 40 yards with no-shoot targets positioned so that I have roughly half an "A" on each target. Of course, you can set them at whatever distance or distances you like and space them out laterally however you prefer.

The diagram is just an example of how you could construct this drill. You don't need a head shot. You can use hard cover instead of no-shoots. Do it up however you like; the important thing is to tailor the shot difficulty as I described.

Procedure:

Start with your hands relaxed at sides. Draw and engage each partial target with two rounds.

Focus:

In addition to marksmanship fundamentals, there is a big element of risk management in this drill. You want to learn just how close to the "A" you can aim without clipping no-shoots.

Goal:

The goal is to set up an extremely challenging scenario, and then learn to consistently shoot it without suffering a miss or no-shoot hit. In terms of time, I like to have a good draw (under 1.5 seconds on a 25-30-yard partial target), and then nice consistent shooting.

Commentary:

Setting up a challenging group of partial targets is something that can challenge a shooter of any level. I get a lot out of this sort of practice every time I do it.

As I pointed out in the focus section, there is a big element of risk management. In a match situation, it isn't acceptable to hit a no-shoot or to have a miss. You simply never want that to happen. That having been said, it isn't acceptable to be dropping all kinds of points either.

What I find helpful is to calculate hit factor on this drill, and then experiment with a few things. You can try spending a bit more time aiming for "A"s and see how that affects your hit factor. You can try hitting the center of the brown target and see how that plays out. Try different strategies and see what happens.

Another thing I like to do is shoot the drill multiple times without pasting any of the targets. My goal is to shoot it five or six times consecutively with no penalties. This ratchets up the difficulty and demands consistency. Again, you can approach it how you want, but for this sort of drill I like to work more in terms of what I am able to consistently pull off than what I can pull off one time in ten.

In any event, the point of this drill is to challenge yourself. Make it tough. I have shot this drill at distances exceeding 60 yards. Yes, it is frustrating. No, you don't see it in matches. The idea here is that you are building a skill level, not necessarily working on things that you are sure you will encounter.

Variations:

I like to vary both starting position and shooting position on this drill.

You can try starting with wrists above shoulders or facing uprange. You may also want to do less conventional start positions like having your gun unloaded and holstered.

The idea behind this is to adapt to the start position, get a good grip on your pistol, and then shoot good points.

You could throw in a barricade or other vision barrier to disrupt your regular stance. The idea there is to build some patience into your shooting. You will need to slow it down just a little bit when shooting from an awkward position. Just let your sights settle back down and then start breaking the next shot.

If you don't want to drag a wall section around, you could try the kneeling position or the prone position. You could even do things like force yourself to move a few yards, then stop in a position and then shoot. Often in matches you will need to run a little bit, then get yourself stopped and make tight shots. This is a good simulation of that.

The measure of success on this drill should always be the level of accuracy you are able to bring to bear. Nothing else really matters.

Fixed Time Standards

If you have been shooting only a few years, you have likely never encountered a proper "fixed time standards." These used to be commonplace at Nationals. Now, they exist only at the Single Stack Nationals and in a few of the more obscure USPSA classifiers. That having been said, these stages are interesting marksmanship challenges, and you can learn a lot from shooting them.

If you aren't aware, the scoring for a fixed time stage is different than a conventional stage. There is no hit factor. It isn't scored points divided by time. Instead, these stages allocate a par time to you, and you simply accumulate as many points as you can in that amount of time. There isn't a penalty associated with shooting a miss. This makes the scoring really easy; you just add up all the points that you got on the targets, and that is your score for the stage. Of course, you aren't allowed to shoot any shots after the par time has elapsed, or to shoot extra shots (without penalty).

The change in the scoring system for these stages creates some really interesting phenomenon. The pace is essentially dictated to you. You draw, and then use up all the time you have available to you to shoot. Spend the time you have to aim the shots as best you can. There is no point in finishing early, because you don't get any reward for it. Depending on how demanding the time limit is, you may find yourself with ample time to shoot, or you may find yourself really rushed. **The bottom line is, you are pulled along at whatever pace is set for you.**

Fixed Time Standards A

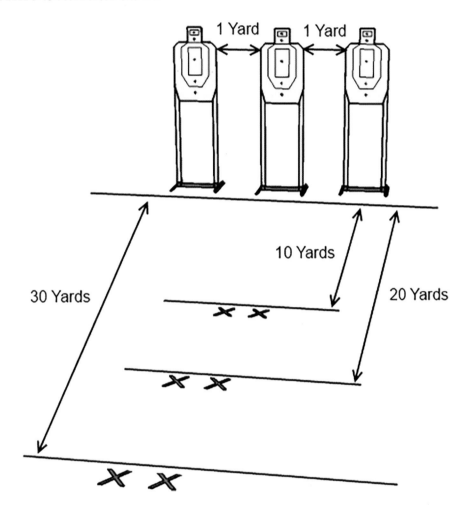

Date:	Par Time:	Notes:
	NA	
	NA	
	NA	
	NA	
	NA	
	NA	
	NA	
	NA	
	NA	
	NA	

Procedure:

This is a multiple-string drill. The start position for every string is hands relaxed at sides. The par time for each string is four seconds. Overtime shots should be assessed a penalty per the current edition USPSA rulebook.

- <u>String 1</u>: From the 30-yard line, engage each target with two rounds freestyle.
- <u>String 2</u>: From the 20-yard line, engage each target with two rounds, strong hand only.
- <u>String 3</u>: From the 10-yard line, engage each target with two rounds, weak hand only.

Focus:

Shoot as many points as you can. Shoot at the pace dictated to you and learn to make it work for you.

Goal:

I think 80 points scoring minor and 85 points scoring major is reasonable for this.

Commentary:

This is an "easy" fixed time standards that I worked up for people that haven't really shot this sort of thing before. Of course, you may think that this is an extraordinarily difficult shooting test, and in many respects it is. However, this is *far* easier than most of the fixed time shooting tests I have seen in actual USPSA competition.

I recommend trying this whole thing at the beginning of a practice session as a bit of a test. You can then work on each string of fire individually. I like to take a few runs at one of the strings to get a feel for it, then move on to the next one. When you are far enough back from the targets that it is tough to see the holes, I recommend pasting the target every single string. Surprising things can happen when you are shooting from 20 or 30 yards, and you want to be sure that you are seeing things in your sight picture. If you shoot a miss, you should know it immediately. You don't want to be surprised when you walk down to score.

Another thing that bears mentioning is learning to "pace" your shots properly. Generally speaking, in USPSA it is a bad idea to try to match some specific pace. You just shoot the shots at your natural speed, and that is the end of it. Sure, you want to improve during practice, but in an actual match situation you just show up and shoot. It is an interesting challenge that you essentially are stripped of shooting the speed you are comfortable and instead forced to shoot a predetermined pace. This can be a useful skill at higher levels of USPSA, when you may want to "push" on a stage or on a particular group of targets. By "push," I mean shooting those targets just a little bit more aggressively than you normally would. This can be useful if you want to pick a very aggressive sequence on a moving target or something like that. It is nice to "push" but still be in control of what is happening. Instead of just slinging rounds with no control, you instead see where everything is going without giving yourself enough time to drive perfect "A"s on everything.

In any event, working with fixed time standards can give you a helpful push in some really great ways.

Variations:

If you like, you can add in a few more variables to make things a bit tougher. You can try adding in a reload on the freestyle string and then giving yourself an extra second on the par time. A reload will make things a bit more challenging, requiring you to be able to get a good grip back on your pistol, and then make more accurate shots.

You might also want to try adding some no-shoots to the targets. You can place them however you feel is reasonable. I wouldn't adjust the par time, but I would change your expectation of points, depending on how you position the no-shoots. Turning these targets into partials will help you refine your point of aim vs. point of impact, especially at 30 yards!

Fixed Time Standards B

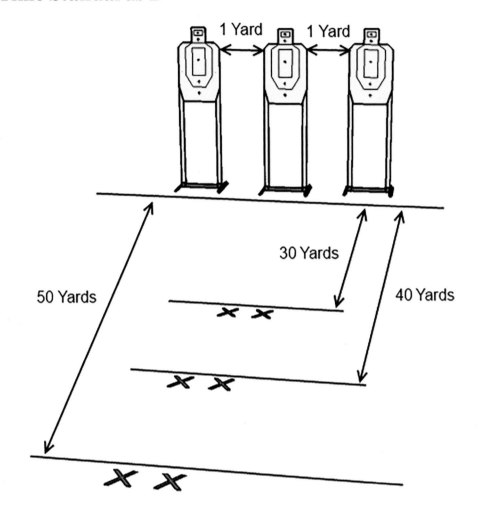

Date:	Par Time:	Notes:
	NA	
	NA	
	NA	
	NA	
	NA	
	NA	
	NA	
	NA	
	NA	
	NA	

Procedure:

This is a multiple-string drill. The start position for every string is wrists above shoulders. The par time for each string is six seconds. Overtime shots should be assessed a penalty per the current edition USPSA rulebook.

- <u>String 1</u>: From the 50-yard line, engage each target with two rounds freestyle.
- <u>String 2</u>: From the 40-yard line, engage each target with two rounds, strong hand only.
- <u>String 3</u>: From the 30-yard line, engage each target with two rounds, weak hand only.

Focus:

Learning to control your shooting and execute fundamentals under serious time pressure.

Goal:

Obtaining 75 points is very reasonable for minor, and 80 points is very achievable for major scoring.

Commentary:

This drill is the big brother of "Fixed Time Standards A." Fundamentally, nothing changes. Realistically, this is a much stiffer challenge.

The key to success on this one is to use the time you have effectively. Don't be lazy about your draw; execute it quickly. You want to save as much time for the noisy stuff as possible.

When you are shooting, be sure you take a close look at the timer. If you aren't using up all the time you have, you may want to consider a pace change. If you are flatly unable to hang all the hits on the cardboard in the time you have, you may want to consider going with "Fixed Time Standards A" until you get that down, and then step up to this drill.

Pay careful attention to your point of aim/impact at 50 yards, especially. You need to hold in the right spot on the target, otherwise you start giving away a lot more points than you have to.

At the end of the day, this drill is about making the best of a bad situation. It is nearly impossible to shoot all 90 points given the time constraints you have, but you want to learn what you can expect with some degree of regularity. You can learn to operate under tight time pressure for some seriously challenging shots.

Variations:

This is identical to "Fixed Time Standards A."

If you like, you can add in a few more variables to make things a bit tougher. You can try adding in a reload on the freestyle string, and then giving yourself an extra second on the par time. A reload will make things a bit more challenging, requiring you to be able to get a good grip back on your pistol and then make more accurate shots.

You might also want to try adding some no-shoots to the targets. You can place them however you feel is reasonable. I wouldn't adjust the par time, but I would change your expectation of points, depending on how you position the no-shoots. Turning these targets into partials will help you refine your point of aim vs. point of impact, especially at 50 yards!

Chapter 4
TRANSITION DRILLS

It might seem odd to some that there is a section just for target transitions. This is new, not something done before this edition of *Skills & Drills.* The logic behind the other groups of drills is probably self-evident. The logic behind breaking out the transition drills into their own section might not be.

The thing to understand is that for most shooters that are already proficient (B or A class), the thing they need to master in order to really move up is usually target transition speed. Many shooters don't have a clear understanding how to engage targets more quickly, and in a speed shooting sport that is going to hold them back. Mastering

these drills is how you shoot faster, it's that simple.

In addition to being very important, target transitions is the thing that is most commonly trained improperly during dryfire. When you work on trigger control or reloads, it is very easy to know if you are doing it correctly or not. Target transitions are a bit easier to do improperly.

So just to reiterate why transitions need to have their own section in this book, they are commonly messed up during dryfire and they are very important for people to master if they want to shoot faster. Work on these drills, master them, and move up.

Basic Transitions

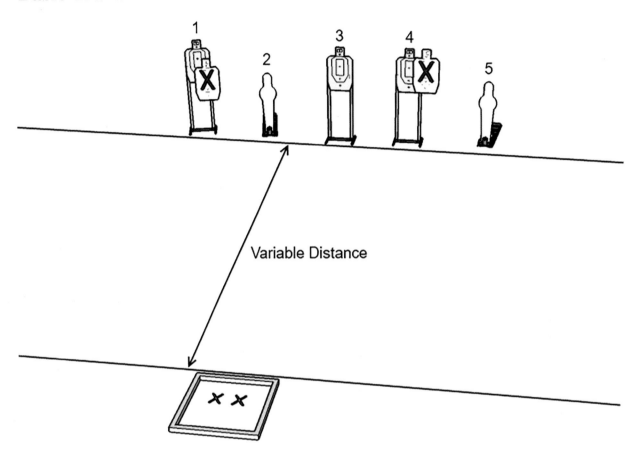

Date:	Par Time:	Notes:
	NA	
	NA	
	NA	
	NA	
	NA	
	NA	
	NA	
	NA	
	NA	
	NA	

Variable Setup:

This is a "variable setup" drill. I outline a concept for a drill, and then you can construct it based on your own situation. Do not attempt to recreate the diagram.

Setup Notes:

This drill requires you to set up targets between 5 and 15 yards. Do not make any target so challenging in terms of difficulty that you feel you need to take excessive care when engaging it. Make sure you have the targets set up so you can see all the targets from one view. No wide transitions, please. Those are covered in a different drill.

Procedure:

Engage each target. Vary the start position between hands relaxed at sides and wrists above shoulders. Vary the direction you start facing as well. Start squarely facing downrange, start squarely facing uprange, and so on.

Focus:

Transition as aggressively as you can without making common transition errors.

Goal:

The goal is to drive your gun aggressively and precisely from target to target.

Commentary:

I recommend you start your target transition training on this drill. Don't set things up too wild and crazy. No targets far away or extremely partial. No wide transitions. Just set up a "normal" shooting scenario.

I also think that you should consciously decide what type of sight picture you require on each target in your scenario. Decide whether you are going to shoot that particular target sight focused or target focused. If you aren't sure then, feel free to do a bit of experimentation to figure out what works best on each target.

As you work through the drill, you should watch for common transition errors. Make sure you aren't pushing the gun too hard during the transition. If you see it go past a target, and then need to wait for the gun to come back, then you will know that you are committing this error. Also pay attention so that the gun goes to the center of the target you are engaging.

The phrase I have in my head when working on transitions is "shoot sooner, not faster." It isn't about how quickly you are jamming the trigger. What you should be thinking about is getting started as soon as possible on each target. Do not "sit on" a good sight picture. When you "see what you need to see," then it is time to shoot. There can be no delay.

I strongly recommend doing a bit of dry-fire warmup for this drill. Practice transitioning through the targets to find the edge of your ability and go from there.

Wide Transitions

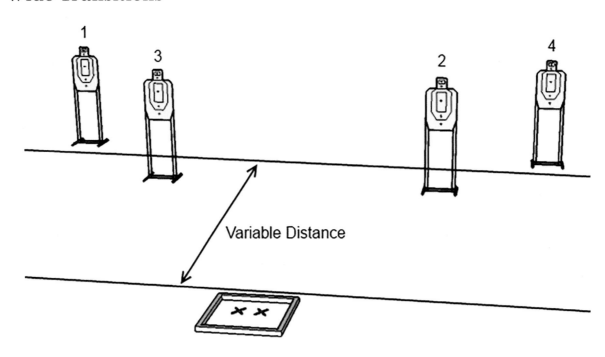

Date:	Par Time:	Notes:
	NA	
	NA	
	NA	
	NA	
	NA	
	NA	
	NA	
	NA	
	NA	
	NA	

Variable Setup:

This is a "variable setup" drill. I outline a concept for a drill and then you can construct it based on your own situation. Do not attempt to recreate the diagram. You should create the scenario outlined in the setup notes. The

"How to Use This Book" section has more information on variable setups.

Setup Notes:

This drill requires a wide bay where you are permitted to shoot nearly 180 degrees. You may not be able to get to 180 degrees in your specific range situation, but the idea is to have as big of a "swing" between the targets as you possibly can. Have a target or two on each side of the bay with your wide transition in the middle of the two sets of targets.

Set the targets at close to mid-range, perhaps 5-15 yards.

Procedure:
Engage each target with two rounds. Vary the start position between hands at sides and wrists above shoulders. Vary the direction you start facing as well. Start squarely facing downrange, start squarely facing up range, and so on.

Focus:
Transition as aggressively as you can without making common transition errors.

Goal:
The goal is to drive your gun aggressively and precisely from target to target.

Commentary:
Extremely wide transitions from target to target are a common obstacle in USPSA matches. You may be surprised how much time is commonly spent on them. It is not uncommon for me to observe target transition times of well over a second, even among above-average shooters. With a good amount of practice, you can reduce your transition times dramatically.

As you work through this livefire exercise, you may want to take some time to look at your technique. Foot placement and body placement is very important when you start looking at driving your times down. The reason that the start position should vary on this drill is that it will force you to constantly evaluate your body position and to figure out the most efficient way to set your feet up.

Generally speaking, I like to be as square as possible to all the targets I am shooting from a position, but that doesn't always hold true. Depending on your range setup, you may need to reposition your feet after shooting one side of the range. You need to experiment with some different things and figure out how to get it done. I strongly recommend working on this drill dryfire first, so you can work out the finer technical points without needing to use ammunition.

You may also want to consider pulling your gun in toward your body as you transition, and then pushing it back out on target. For extreme transitions (120 degrees or more), this technique can be more efficient and accurate. Again, it depends on the specific scenario that you create.

The most common mistake made on this drill will be "overtransitioning." This is when you put in too much muscle as you transition from one group of targets to the next. Be very sensitive to your sight picture as you complete the wide transition. If you see the sights go past your point of aim and then return, you overtransitioned. Be very careful to correct this error by using a bit less force as you move the gun.

Distance Transitions

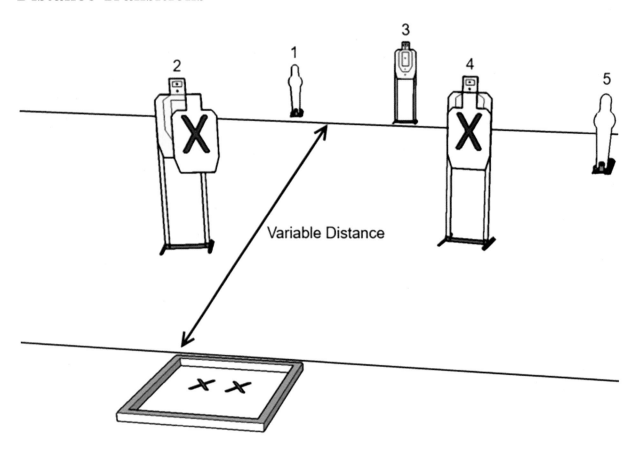

Date:	Par Time:	Notes:
	NA	
	NA	
	NA	
	NA	
	NA	
	NA	
	NA	
	NA	
	NA	
	NA	

Variable Setup:

This is a "variable setup" drill. I outline a concept for a drill and then you can construct it based on your own situation. Do not attempt to recreate the diagram. You should create the scenario outlined in the setup notes. The "How to Use This Book" section has more information on variable setups.

Setup Notes:

This exercise should be set up with a variety of targets, set at varying distances and difficulties. You should experiment with everything from close range to long range, partial targets, and open targets.

Procedure:

Start standing with your hands in any desired position. At the start signal, engage all the targets.

Focus:

The focus of this drill is to be quick on all of the easy targets and be accurate on the distant targets.

Goal:

The goal is to give each target exactly the amount of time and attention it requires, but no more. You want to be able to consistently shoot this exercise in a fast time, but consistently nail the accuracy. In terms of time, you should look to achieve your fastest times on all the different transitions based on your previous training.

Commentary:

This type of practice is essential to people looking to reach the top level.

First, the goal may seem a bit unclear, so I want to lay it out in more detail. The goal time for this exercise is based entirely on your previous training. It all depends on how you set up the targets, but no matter how you set them up, you will have shot targets of that approximate difficulty before. Using your past training, you should have approximate goal times for every transition and split. From that, you can come up with an approximate goal time for the entire exercise. For example, if you have a head box at 10 yards, your previous training may inform you that it takes you approximately 0.8 seconds to transition onto that target, and 0.4 seconds to split on that target. You can then systematically figure out your goal time from information like that.

Another thing I like to do when working on target transitions is to experiment with different aiming methods on different targets. You may like to shoot a certain target with target focus, but why not try shooting with a hard front sight focus? You can always be experimenting with different aiming methods.

At the end of the day, setting up drills like this will help you develop consistency and accuracy on the longer shots, and that will be key for doing well at major matches. It is normally the case at major matches that many shooting positions in a stage will require some sort of distance transition.

Low Targets

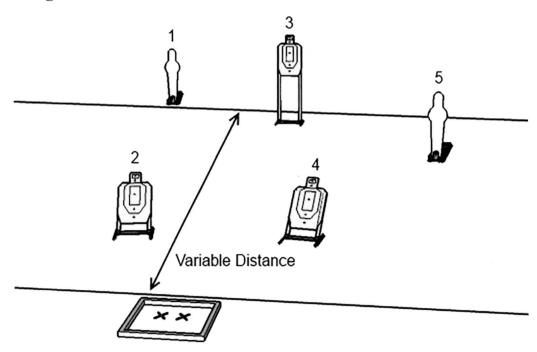

Date:	Par Time:	Notes:
	NA	
	NA	
	NA	
	NA	
	NA	
	NA	
	NA	
	NA	
	NA	
	NA	

Variable Setup:

This is a "variable setup" drill. I outline a concept for a drill and then you can construct it based on your own situation. Do not attempt to recreate the diagram.

Setup Notes:

This drill requires that you have 45-degree angled stands so you can place the targets low, pretty much right at your feet. As usual, create a target scenario similar to the diagram.

Procedure:

Start with your hands relaxed at sides and engage the targets in any desired order. Be sure to experiment with different engagement orders in subsequent attempts.

Focus:

Become proficient at shooting close-range low targets.

Goal:

Be able to transition onto and off of low targets efficiently.

Commentary:

Low targets are something that you will encounter occasionally. I think the primary lesson with them is that you would be surprised how fast they can be shot, but engaging them at maximum speed with confidence will require some practice.

Normally, low targets are just part of a shooting position. You almost always need to address targets at conventional height and longer distance as well. I think the primary consideration here is being comfortable taking those shots in any order. You should be able to

go left to right, right to left, low to high, and high to low. This means you need to be comfortable swinging down aggressively to knock out the low targets, and swinging up aggressively to the high targets. You may find it difficult to swing up to targets both aggressively and accurately. In that situation, I usually just don't push quite as hard coming up to the high targets.

In any event, experimentation is absolutely critical to your success on these targets. Remember, you will be amazed how fast you can really go on those close targets.

Variations:

It is not uncommon for low targets to be placed behind three or four foot tall wall sections, requiring shooters to lean over a little bit to engage them. If you are able to replicate this in your own training, I recommend you try it. There really isn't anything challenging about it if you are tall, but if you are a short-statured shooter, you may find the position challenging or uncomfortable. I have seen some setups like this that actually prevented the shortest shooters from using their sights.

Steel/Paper/Steel

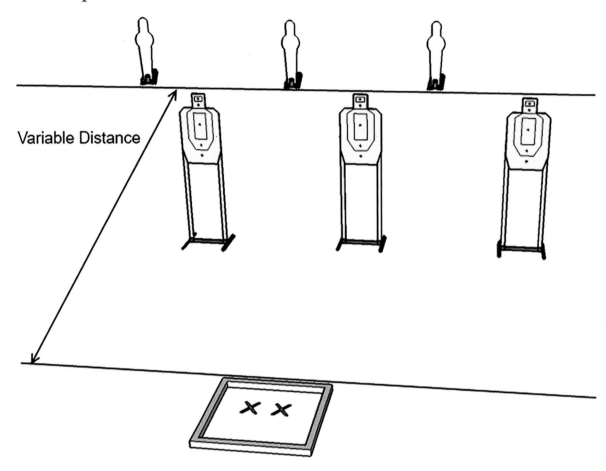

Date:	Par Time:	Notes:
	NA	
	NA	
	NA	
	NA	
	NA	
	NA	
	NA	
	NA	
	NA	
	NA	

Setup Notes:

This is not a standard exercise. Feel free to add or subtract targets as you wish. Adapt to whatever steel targets you have on hand.

Procedure:

Start with your hands in any desired position. At the start signal, engage each target with the appropriate number of rounds. Vary engagement order between left to right, right to left, steel then paper, and paper then steel.

Focus:

The focus here is to transition as aggressively as possible between the targets.

Goal:

The goal is to drive your gun aggressively and precisely from target to target. There should be no delay when transitioning from steel to paper. Call your shots by sight and not sound if at all possible.

Commentary:

This drill is designed to give your transitions on to and off of steel a workout. Many shooters struggle with steel targets, and mixing them in with close-range paper targets only makes matters more difficult. This is a drill to master if you have problems with steel.

The first thing I would do is start thinking about shooting with confidence. A big time waster when engaging steel is any lack of confidence about where your shots are going. You can't wait to hear audible confirmation from the steel; that is way too slow. You are going to need to accurately assess what is happening at the speed of your eyes and your sights. If you need a follow-up shot on a piece of steel, then you should fire it immediately. Minimize any conscious thought during this drill. Transitioning from the steel to the paper is where you will almost certainly be punished if there is any delay. Listening for a hit on the steel target will cost time. Being unsure will cost time.

As you transition from the paper to the steel, think in terms of finesse. Don't slam the gun around hard. Look to the center of the steel you intend to hit and let the gun settle there. Be very sensitive to any overtransitioning!

If you are looking for firm numbers, I can provide a couple for you. Going from steel to paper can be done in under 0.3 seconds if you are aggressive. You can do the reverse in about half a second under good circumstances.

The Accelerator

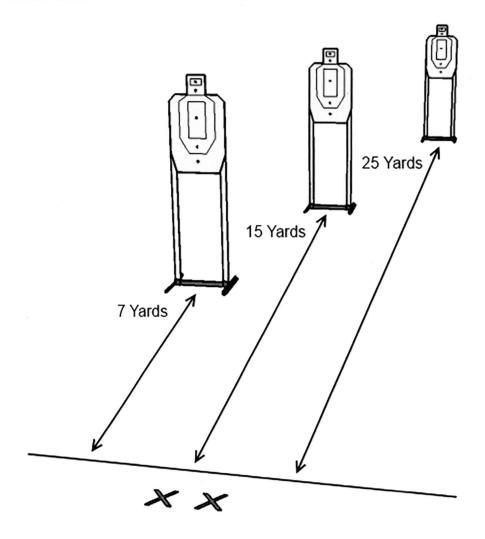

Date:	Par Time:	Notes:
	NA	
	NA	
	NA	
	NA	
	NA	
	NA	
	NA	
	NA	
	NA	
	NA	

Setup Notes:

Set up the targets so that they are perhaps a yard apart laterally as you view them from your shooting position.

Procedure:

Start with your hands relaxed at sides. Engage each target with two rounds, reload, and re-engage each target with an additional two rounds.

Focus:

Learn to "change gears" as you work between targets of different distances/difficulty levels. You should be fast and accurate up close, but take the time you need to get mostly "A"s on the further targets.

Goal:

Being able to consistently shoot this drill in under six seconds with good points (a couple "C"s) is a great goal.

Commentary:

This has been a popular drill over the last couple years, a particular favorite of mine. It seems that no matter what your skill level is, you can always learn something from this.

The whole idea here is to be able to *seamlessly* change gears between targets of different difficultly levels. Maybe you just look through the gun up close, get a hard front sight focus at 25 yards, and do something in the middle at 15 yards. In any event, you need to go between all those modes of shooting without there being a hitch present.

I like to pay careful attention to the timer on this one, especially the split times on each target. If your split times are the same at 7 yards as they are at 25 yards, that should tell you something. (That is a common scenario.) If you don't pick up speed as you go from the back target to the front, something is wrong. You may be shooting everything at "hose" speed, or you may be unable to transition from distance shooting into close-range blasting. In any event, don't trust your ears. Look though the timer and figure out what is actually happening.

The other big issue with this drill is that it doesn't specify what order you should engage the targets. Everyone has different preferences, but I think that most of the more experienced shooters prefer to go far to near on this drill. However, I think you should train opposite of what you prefer. You never know what you will end up doing in a match situation, and you don't want to be hindered by personal preference when it comes time to select appropriate stage tactics.

Also, you should experiment with going different directions in the same string. For example, start far to near, reload, then go near to far. You may find that you like a hybrid method.

Pay particular attention to your draw and reload times. If you have worked through much of the "Standard Practice Setup," you will have a good idea of what you are capable of. Check the timer frequently to make sure you are laying down appropriate draw and reload times.

Variations:

Of course, you can and should vary the start position. Wrists above shoulders and a turning draw are some common options you may want to try.

If you have a particularly high skill level, you may want to change the distances of the targets. You could go 10, 20, and 30 yards instead of the standard distance. It will add a bit of time to the drill, but it will be a bit more demanding in terms of marksmanship.

Distance Changeup

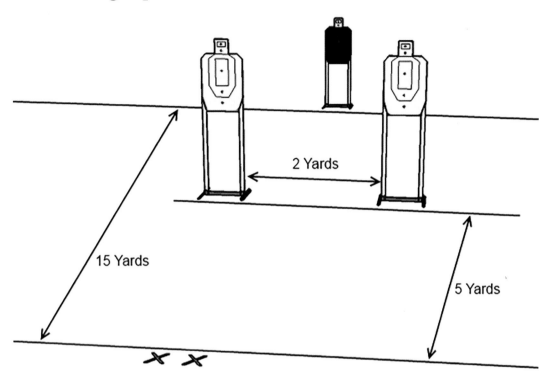

Date:	Par Time:	Notes:
	NA	
	NA	
	NA	
	NA	
	NA	
	NA	
	NA	
	NA	
	NA	
	NA	

Procedure:
Start with your hands relaxed at sides. Engage each target with two rounds.

Focus:
This drill (as the name implies) is all about working between targets of varying difficulty levels.

Goal:

I think getting under three seconds on this drill is a very achievable goal. You want to hit that time *and* the head box with regularity.

Commentary:

This drill is certainly challenging. I have two goals here.

1. Be fast on the close targets.
2. Be accurate on the head box.

On the close target, I do the usual "look through the gun" thing and drive the gun as hard as possible. It is important to find the center of the close targets with your eyes, and then drive the gun just to that spot. At only five yards, it is possible to shoot all "A"s pretty much as fast as you can pull the trigger, so I like to bear that in mind during my own training.

If points are dropped on the close targets, it is likely that one of two things happened. If I miss my grip when I draw, the gun will come to the target without the sights in alignment. If the gun comes up to the target wrong, then I end up dropping points. The other common issue is to "drag" shots off the target, or get on the trigger before the gun gets to the center of the target. So essentially, I focus on hitting my grip at high speed and getting the gun into the "A" of the target before I break the shots.

On the distant target, the most common error I see is firing the second shot before the gun settles back down out of recoil. It is very common to "sling" shots over the top of the head box in this fashion. Patience is absolutely key on this target. One other thing that helps is to go for the "A" box in the head. Don't just try to hit the head anywhere, drive shots into that "A" zone. That way, if you make a mistake and miss the "A," you are at least likely to still hit the "B" and avoid a miss penalty.

I recommend you shoot this drill in every order. Go left to right, right to left, near to far, and far to near. This is just to give you a bit of practice with your "gear changes." I think you will likely find that your best scores come from going left to right or right to left, but you may be surprised that they aren't the best by much.

Variations:

Of course, you can and should vary the start position. Wrists above shoulders and a turning draw are some common options you may want to try.

You may also prefer to use a steel target in place of the head shot. That is perfectly acceptable, but realize it does make the drill a bit easier.

If your skill level is not up to making a 15-yard head shot during a speed shooting drill, you can move that target in a bit closer until you get better.

Chapter 5
STANDARD EXERCISES

The drills in this section are designed to improve your core USPSA skills. Things such as drawing, reloading, and split times.

This section contains all the boilerplate USPSA drills that you would expect from a book like this, and with good reason. **These drills work.** I will clearly explain the "benchmark" times and how to achieve them. For example, it isn't easy to shoot an "El Presidente" in less than five seconds, but it is a straightforward sort of challenge. It can be done by pretty much any shooter, with pretty much any gear.

It is frequently the case that I will teach a class and ask people about their shooting. "What is your draw?" is a frequent question. When I ask a question like that, hopefully people are able to produce some sort of number. Ideally, people should know what sort of first shot time they can expect under all sorts of different parameters. What sort of parameters, you wonder?

Things like:

- How much warm-up practice did they do?
- What is the distance to the target?
- Did they shoot a guaranteed "A" or was it a "hoper" shot?
- Was it the first shot of a multiple-shot drill?
- What was the start position?

- How hot is it outside?
- And so on. . .

The questions one could ask are virtually endless, but the point is, you can (and should) know about how long it takes for you to draw and shoot a given target under some given set of circumstances. The same goes for a number of other actions. You ought to know how much time there will be between one target and another. You ought to know how long it takes for you to reload your gun and engage the next target. The list goes on.

You may be thinking at this point . . . *why?*

It is a good question. What difference does it make what your draw is? It is what it is. You go to a match and just go your speed. It doesn't make a difference if you know what your speed is or not. You just do your thing and the cards fall where they may. Now, that is a reasonable position, but there is more to the story.

The fact is, I rarely meet someone that has a detailed and accurate perception of how long things take them, and is at the same time very slow. When people pay attention to the timer during their training, they naturally tend to change their behavior. It is a well-documented phenomenon that when people know they are being observed, they tend to change their behavior. You can make this work for you by simply paying attention to your own shooting and starting to figure out how long stuff takes you.

Another important thing that bears mentioning here is that one really important element of effective stage breakdown is knowing how long things take you to perform. If you know how long things take, then you can make better decisions when you are presented with a few different choices. If you don't know, then you are left to either guess or follow the rest of the pack on your squad.

All the drills in this section are *repeatable*. If you set up a classifier or a particular skills test, you are going to be able to set that up three months down the line and see if anything has changed. This is a really important tool! Use it.

In addition to having a repeatable set of drills, I also have some goal times that are appropriate for the iron sighted divisions (maybe a bit slanted toward Production Division). The idea is to be able to perform to the standards that I set for you. If you can do that, you are in good stead. In later sections, I will describe the documentation process in detail. For now, just know that all of these drills are standardized and, thus, repeatable to set up.

Becoming a GM

When I came into USPSA, I immediately was able to make Grand Master. Some people thought this was a function of natural talent. It wasn't.

I was able to do this by setting up a few classifier stages, and then figuring out what it took to shoot a 100 percent score on them. I learned how fast I needed to draw, how fast I needed to reload, and how fast I needed to pull the trigger. My training wasn't solely about going as fast as

I could or shooting like my hair was on fire. I had a set of goals. After I knew what I needed to do, I set up drills to accomplish that.

The fact is, I used a narrow set of repeatable drills. All of those drills, and some more, are included in this section. If you want to become a GM, then it is just a matter of making the decision to do it and forcing yourself to meet the challenge.

Some people may feel like this is in some way unethical or maybe just silly. It is often the case that people will want to get to the GM level, and then get a classification bump from match performance. Other people are afraid of being labeled a "paper GM" because they engaged in "grandbagging." This isn't what I am telling you to do. I am not telling you to practice a narrow set of drills and then get a classification that you can't perform to. I am telling you that you should become a Grand Master. You can learn to draw quickly, reload quickly, and shoot fast and consistently. If you can develop those core skills, then the run and gun elements that make you great on a field course will come much more easily. This system works, I promise you.

GM Core Skills

If you want to become a GM, you might be wondering what it is you have to do. I have some numbers for you.

You want to be able to do the following under match pressure with a 95 percent success rate. You want every shot you fire to be an "A" or a close "C."

All of these numbers are pulled from multiple-shot drills. It may seem odd to point that out, but if you have ever gone to the range and practiced drawing the gun quickly and slinging one round at a target, you know that it is easy to get lucky when you have only a one round drill. If you fire a few more rounds during a drill or exercise, it really reduces the effect of "getting lucky."

The following times are all practice times that you should be able to hit with regularity. Start position is hands relaxed at sides.

Distance: 7 yards
1-second draw
2-second "Bill Drill"
2-second "Blake Drill"
0.2-second splits
0.2-second target transitions (with one yard between each target)

Distance: 10 yards
5-second "El Presidente"
0.2-second split
1.2-second reload
1.1-second draw

Distance: 15 yards
0.25-second split
1.4-second reload
1.2-second draw

Some people may look at those numbers and think they don't sound that tough. In a sense, that is true. Many shooters I know that practice for just a few minutes are able to produce a one second draw at seven yards. Many people shoot something like 0.2 splits on close-range targets with very little effort. There are more

than a few C class shooters that are able to hit some elements of this occasionally.

It is simply a matter of regular practice and takes a bit of desire to be a little bit more consistent and systematic during your practice. Once you do that, becoming a GM is almost inevitable.

With just three target stands, you can run a large variety of drills. There is pretty much no limit to what you can do. To that end, I have included a standardized practice setup along with a plethora of drills. There are goal times for everything, and all of them are in a quick-reference table at the end of the "Standard Practice Setup" section. If you train to shoot "A"s within these times, you will quite likely be a Master or Grand Master shooter in short order in Limited or Production. Open shooters will need to be a bit quicker.

Standard Practice Setup

The drills in this section are a bit different than other parts of the book. All the drills are run on one standardized practice setup. Of course, you can run lots of different drills from different distances and that sort of thing, but all of that can be done without moving the targets around. You may also notice that the drills in this section look very similar to some classifier stages that you may encounter. That certainly isn't an accident.

Simply put, I have a catalog of drills here that you can run using three targets that are set one yard apart. You can run drills anywhere from 3 yards to as far as 50 yards. I have included as much commentary as possible to help convey the best depiction regarding what these drills should look like.

Standard Practice Setup

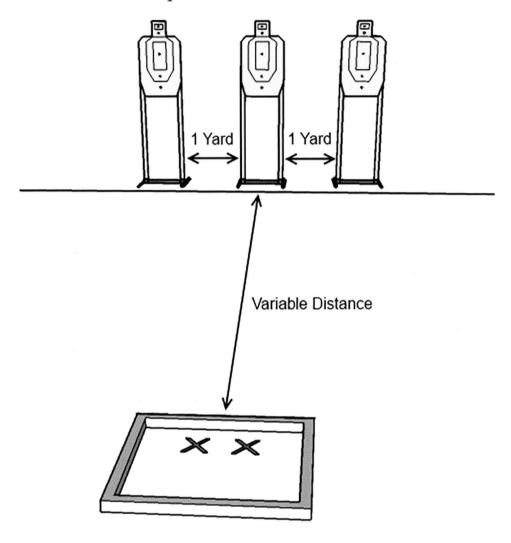

Date:	Par Time:	Notes:
	NA	
	NA	
	NA	
	NA	
	NA	
	NA	
	NA	
	NA	
	NA	
	NA	

You may notice that the distance reads "variable." The reason is that you can obviously shoot drills from many different distances without changing the layout of the targets.

I have a quick reference table below of the drills and distances. In the following pages, I have a description of the drills and some commentary.

Distance	3 yards	5 yards	7 yards	10 yards	15 yards	20 yards	25 yards	50 yards
Doubles	1.0	1.1	1.2	1.3	1.5	1.8	2.0	3.0
Bill Drill	1.7	1.8	2.0	2.2	2.5	3.2	4.0	6.0
Blake Drill	NA	1.8	2.0	2.2	2.5	NA	NA	NA
Singles	1.2	1.3	1.4	1.6	1.8	2.2	2.6	NA
El Prez	NA	NA	4.8	5.0	6.0	7.0	8.0	12
Four Aces	2.2	2.3	2.5	2.7	3.0	3.5	4.0	6.0
SHO	2.0	2.5	3.0	3.5	4.0	5.0	6.0	10
WHO	3.0	3.5	4.0	4.5	5.0	6.0	8.0	12
Bill/Reload	4.0	4.2	4.5	5.0	6.0	7.0	7.5	12
Heads	NA	3.0	3.5	4.0	5.0	5.5	6.0	NA
Crisscross	NA	5.0	5.5	6.0	7.0	8.0	NA	NA

The start position for all of these goal times is facing downrange with your hands relaxed at sides. The one exception to this is the "El Prez."

Doubles

One standard exercise that I enjoy and get a lot of benefit from is drawing and firing two rounds into a target. I have tried shooting only one round into a target, but I really don't like that. I really get the sense that firing the second round "keeps you honest" with your grip and your technique. If you don't need to fire a follow on shot, it makes it a lot easier to simply whip the gun out quickly and go for a lucky "A" hit.

3 Yards

Three yards is basically within spitting distance of a target. This may seem like an absurdly close range to practice, but there is

certainly a lot to be learned from this. I think it is important to realize how little traditional sight focus you need at extreme close range like this. Drawing and firing two rounds can be accomplished in under one second with a little bit of practice. Many people can go faster—a lot faster. Times lower than 0.8 seconds are certainly possible on this drill.

I like to focus on a couple things during this drill. First, having really relaxed arms can help you move quickly and smoothly from the holster out to the target. If you tense up, you are in trouble. I also like to see just how little "sight picture" I can get away with and still shoot "A"s. Seeing the outline of the gun on the target is usually enough.

5 Yards

Shooting doubles at five yards is similar to three yards, you just need a little bit more confirmation of your gun's alignment with the "A" zone. It is amazing how little time that confirmation adds to the draw stroke . . . just a few hundredths of a second are required. For me, seeing the fiber dot come onto the target as I draw is usually enough to get me "A" hits. A time of 1.1 seconds is a very reasonable goal for two solid "A" hits at this distance.

7 Yards

The seven-yard double is a good place to sort out your draw time. This distance certainly requires a lot more in the way of a sight picture than closer distances, but there is no time to screw around either. Personally, I get a good grip on my pistol, push up to the target, and when I see my front fiber visible through the rear notch, I cut loose and start shooting. A reasonable goal is 1.2 seconds. This is the distance where I make sure I can consistently crack one second for a draw. If you can't do it consistently in practice, you are going to have a tough time doing it in a match situation.

10 Yards

Ten yards is where you start having to worry a bit more about getting good sight alignment. At this distance, draw times tend to drift up over a second, and there isn't really anything wrong with that. It is important to let the sights settle into the "A" zone before you start slinging lead. A reasonable goal here is 1.3 seconds.

15 Yards

At 15 yards, things start getting really complicated. This distance is close enough that a competent shooter can still pull fast split times, but far enough away that having your sights misaligned will cause some serious problems. Interestingly, I can use either a target focus or a front sight focus at this distance, and it doesn't seem to affect the results a whole lot. A reasonable goal here is 1.5 seconds.

20 Yards

At 20 yards, the pendulum starts to swing more heavily toward deliberate shooting and a hard front sight focus. A reasonable goal time to shoot two "A"s is 1.8 seconds. If you want to make that time, it is key to draw at the same speed you would up close, and then just spend the extra time refining your sight picture and carefully working the trigger. Since I use a double-action gun, I start really paying attention to getting a smooth press on the first shot. It is easy to end up with a "D" or a miss just from crappy trigger control. I don't want to see that happen.

25 Yards

This is the same drill that was included earlier in the book, and for good reason. To hit "A"s at 25 yards, you need to do everything right. Two seconds is a reasonable goal, but it can be done much faster.

50 Yards

If you feel up to it (and you feel your equipment can do it), then two "A"s at 50 yards is something you should certainly try. When I am shooting this drill, it feels like I spend an eternity aiming and working the trigger for the first shot. In reality, it doesn't take as long as it feels like, but the perception of the time spent is something that you should get used to. When you are shooting matches and really aiming for the tough shots, it can cause you to rush and shoot misses if you aren't used to spending the time you need to make the longer shots.

Also, at 50 yards I really feel it helps to remind myself that I am firing two carefully aimed shots. If you think of it as firing a pair of shots, then your second shot will almost certainly be errant. I set three seconds as the goal time for this drill. Don't kid yourself, this isn't about how fast you can go; it is about firing accurate shots.

Ben firing "Doubles"

Bill Drills

"Bill Drills" are a multipurpose drill. There is a lot you can get out of it. The procedure for the "Bill Drill" is to draw and fire six rounds into the target. At closer ranges, you should strive for all "A" zone hits. At longer ranges, the occasional close "C" is no big deal.

At closer ranges, you will see that this drill tests two things, primarily.

First, your draw is obviously a huge component of your time. You need a fast draw, and you need that draw to end in a correct grip. If you miss your grip, you will have a hard time doing well on the drill. You may have to adjust your grip when you are already on target, or shoot slowly as you fight to keep your sights in the center of the target, or maybe you will just drop a lot of points. In any event, getting your grip right is extremely important.

Second, the "Bill Drill" is a test of staying relaxed. If your body tenses up, you lose the ability to draw quickly or to run the trigger fast. You may suffer some "trigger freeze;" where you try to pull the trigger, but then can't do it because you did not release it enough to reset.

At longer ranges, this really turns into a trigger control test.

If it sounds like there is a theme to this drill, where you learn what it takes to shoot "A"s at different distances and make it happen quickly, you are right on the money. This drill is a great way to learn. Work down to the goal times as quickly as you can, and then work within the goal time to hit the "A" box. You will need to have a highly developed draw to be able to make it happen. I would recommend working on "Doubles" before you progress to this drill.

Ben shooting a "Bill Drill"

3 Yards

As I pointed out, at close range you need to stay relaxed. There is usually a temptation to tense up and try to go really fast. It will not take you long to figure out that the harder you push and harder you try, the tougher it is to stay relaxed. The key is just to let your arms work smoothly to bring the gun up to the target. As soon as the gun is aligned, you should be able to start shooting. A reasonable goal time for this is 1.7 seconds. That may sound fast (and it is), but remember that you will hardly need to aim, and will be able to shed lead as fast as you can pull the trigger.

Five Yards

Five yards is still very close. You should be able to fire the gun as fast as you can pull the trigger and still hold every shot in the "A" zone. I like to experiment with grip pressure quite a bit. I get the best trigger speed if I don't crush down that hard with my strong hand, but with my weak hand I get better control if I crank down on the gun. A very reasonable time at this distance is 1.8 seconds.

7 Yards

This is the standard distance for a "Bill Drill." I suppose you could say you need a good smooth draw, a solid grip, and a trigger finger that is able to keep up. Try not to tense up! Two seconds is a very reasonable goal for this distance. That breaks down to a one second draw and 0.2 second splits.

This is one of those tests that is great to try when you are "cold." If you can hit the first six rounds out of your gun for the day into a seven-yard "A" zone in less than two seconds, you are doing very well indeed.

10 Yards

I have selected 2.2 seconds as a reasonable goal time for this distance. The extra time comes from letting your sights settle down just a little bit as you come onto the target and perhaps backing off on the trigger speed. At 10 yards, most people can't shoot as fast as they can pull the trigger and still hit all "A"s. I certainly can't. The idea here is to back off just enough to hold your shots in the "A" zone, but not so much you can't make the goal time.

15 Yards

For good reason, 15 yards has been described by the great Brian Enos as "the ultimate distance." It is just far enough that you need to aim pretty hard at the target to hit the center, but not so far that you can't really "get on the gas" when you are shooting. This is why I have selected 2.5 seconds as the goal time, and believe me there is no time to screw around. You need a fast draw and fast shooting, but you still need some control over that shooting.

20 Yards

At 20 yards, you may find yourself needing to muscle the gun back down in the "A" zone of the target. If you shoot too relaxed, you may not have the amount of control over the gun you need to return it to the target and fire the shots to make the goal time of 3.2 seconds. Pay careful attention to your trigger control and drive some "A" hits out there.

25 Yards

I discussed this distance in the previous section, marksmanship training.

50 Yards

I discussed this distance in the previous section, marksmanship training.

Blake Drill

The "Blake Drill" takes its name from Blake Miguez. This isn't because he invented the drill. It is because the drill was invented for others to emulate his shooting. Blake is known for extremely fast target transitions and fast hosing.

In any event, this drill is supposed to help you develop that blazing speed across the targets.

The procedure for the drill is to draw and fire two rounds on each target. The interesting thing is that the goal time is the same as the "Bill Drill" goal time. So, from seven yards you still have the two-second goal time, even though you are splitting your shots across three targets rather than dumping them into one.

The standard distance for this drill is the seven-yard line. From there, I think two seconds is a very reasonable goal time. That breaks down into a one-second draw, and then five splits in the remaining second. This should sound exactly like a "Bill Drill."

The way I personally learned to shoot this drill, and the way I still practice it today, is that I force myself to fire the shots within the goal time, and then focus on getting the gun from one target to the next. Essentially, I program my trigger finger to shoot 0.2 splits, and then force myself to get the gun to the next target before it goes off again.

Obviously, this would be a stupid thing to do in a competition, but as a training exercise it is valuable. It reminds me of the footage I have seen of Olympic swimmers in a pool being pulled along by a machine. The device motors them through the pool at a faster speed than they could ever swim, but in the process, they learn about how to position their bodies and get through the water more efficiently. I think the same idea can work for shooters. By forcing yourself to make that goal time, you learn to drive the gun quickly from target to target.

In any event, as you work the drill, you will probably find that the problem isn't squirting bullets at the targets quickly, it is getting "A" hits. In order to make this happen, I have found there are a few things you need to do right.

First, you need to get a good grip on your pistol. If you have a nice consistent grip, the gun will aim wherever you look . . . especially at the close ranges that this drill is intended for. If you miss your grip on the pistol, it will likely end up pointing slightly in the wrong direction. **If you bring the pistol up to eye level, and you see the front sight isn't sitting in the notch, you probably missed your grip.** This is essentially an issue that is most easily fixed during dryfire practice. Until you fix it in dryfire practice, it is almost a waste of bullets to come out and bang on this drill when it relies so heavily on your "index" (ability to look to a spot and have the sights show up in alignment on that spot).

Another common issue is to "drag" the gun off the target you are currently shooting, or "dragging" rounds onto the target you are transitioning to. If you start going fast, this simply will happen. Ideally, your gun should go to the center of the target and stop, then move quickly to the center of the next target, and stop again. If you try to "sweep" the targets, as in keeping the gun moving and pulling the trigger the whole time, you are likely to get some bad hits . . . especially on the center target.

When you make mistakes like this, keep in mind that slowing down probably isn't going to be the ticket to improvement. The "Blake Drill" is designed to help you learn to transition the gun aggressively between targets. Mistakes will happen. If you only shoot the drill at your comfortable pace, you probably aren't learning anything.

During classes, shooters frequently have trouble with this drill. They make the aforementioned mistakes frequently. The thing to remember here is that you can learn a lot shooting this drill, but the most important thing to learn is how to drive your eyes to the exact spot on the target where you want the gun to go. You can accomplish this quickly with some practice. A couple hundredths of a second between targets is very achievable on this drill, and you will need to do it if you want to have any hope of hitting that two-second goal time at seven yards.

One note on this drill, since it is a target transition drill, it is made difficult by adding in degrees of swing between the targets. I don't think it makes a great deal of sense to shoot this drill from a long distance, because

with the targets only separated by one yard, there isn't really any swinging that needs to be done between targets. I wouldn't bother shooting this drill past about 15 yards. In any case, the goal time is the same as the "Bill Drill" goal time.

Singles (One on Each)

The procedure for this drill is simple. Draw and engage each target with one round from the specified distance.

If you are looking to push your target transitions to be a bit faster, then working on shooting one round only on each target can be a big help. If you are shooting one round instead of two at each target, it essentially means that you feel like you need to keep the gun moving the whole time in order to have a fast time. At the same time, you want to strive for "A"s, not just land a hit anywhere on the cardboard. This is a collision of opposing forces, and it can be tough to deal with it.

3 Yards

I have selected a goal time of 1.2 seconds for this distance. That doesn't leave you a whole lot of time to screw around. If you draw any slower than about a 0.8, you are going to have a tough time making that 1.2-second run happen.

I like to shoot this drill from this short distance to remind myself of how little sight picture I can actually get away with, and how much transition speed is actually attainable. These targets are very close, and need to be shot so quickly that I find myself tensing up a lot.

Another thing that bears mentioning is that the distance is close, but there is actually more transitioning at this distance, because the targets are separated by more degrees of swing when you stand closer to them. So, you need to push the gun fast to get a good time.

5 Yards

At five yards, you don't need a whole lot more sight picture than you do at three yards. However, I find that I am much more successful if I pay special attention to making sure I see my sights pretty well on the first target. After that, simply getting my eyes to the next target and pushing the gun along with them should be enough to hit the targets in the center.

I selected 1.3 seconds as a goal time. This essentially gives you that extra tenth of a second (compared to three yards) to get things lined up just a bit better for the first shot.

7 Yards

At seven yards, things get interesting. I selected 1.4 seconds as the goal time for this distance. I think most people will find it easier to be fast on this drill than to be accurate. If you get in a hurry and really start cracking rounds off downrange, you will likely have bad hits. It is difficult to shoot all "A"s consistently at this distance. You will not have time to let the gun settle into the targets, and that is what makes this tough. Pretty much anyone can hang hits on the paper fast, but your goal is to get all the points available, not just try to luck out and get everything in the "A" zone once out of 10 tries. Try to develop the control and the discipline to get the sights to the target, and

then break the shot without spending any time refining that sight picture.

10 Yards

The goal time at 10 yards is 1.6 seconds. I suspect you will find that by the time you get back to this distance, the time isn't really as demanding as getting all "A" hits. Really, letting the sight come down on to each target and making sure you drive "A"s is the key. It requires a ton of discipline to make it happen, but the effort is certainly worth it.

15 Yards

At 15 yards, the most important element, time-wise, is going to come down to your draw speed. It is important to draw at a "3-yard pace," and only spend extra time on the sights making sure the gun gets lined up properly. Personally, I really start looking for a sharp front sight focus on this drill at this distance.

20 Yards

At 20 yards, it makes for some challenging trigger control. The time limit for this distance is 2.2 seconds. There should be plenty of time to get a good sharp sight picture for each shot. Again, if you have trouble making the time limit, the first thing I would look at is your draw speed. An acceptable draw at this distance is 1.3 to 1.4 seconds, so if you aren't making that time, consider working up your draw.

25 Yards

At 25 yards, there is hardly even a transition between the targets. You just need to bump the sights over a little bit to the next target, let them settle, and then carefully break the next shot. The goal time is 2.6 seconds.

El Presidente

"El Presidente," or "El Prez," is one of those famous drills that pretty much everyone has heard of. It is also a USPSA classifier stage. In any event, this is a very popular "benchmark" drill.

The procedure is simple. Starting with your wrists above your shoulders while facing uprange, turn, draw, and engage each target with two rounds. Reload, and reengage each target with an additional two rounds, for a total of 12 rounds fired.

The standard distance for this drill is 10 yards. So, any discussion of the drill will usually mean that we are talking about that specific distance. There are some popular variations, such as the IDPA classifier, which uses a two yard spacing between the targets, and a tactical version where you draw from concealment. There are many versions of the "El Presidente" drill.

In any event, the "El Prez" is an iconic drill, but it is also a very useful drill. I recommend paying particular attention to the times and hits you can lay down on this drill.

For the record, the goal times for "El Prez" are (as usual) times that I think are reasonable for a solid M or GM shooter. Don't think that this is the end of the road. Over the years, competitors have pushed the times down, and now the top level shooters in the sport can accomplish some amazing stuff. At 10 yards, the goal time I have listed is five seconds. That is a sporty time, but the top level shooters

I know can consistently shoot this drill in the mid four second range during practice (with only a few "C" zone hits!). Most of them can break four seconds when they decide to "go fast," and some of them can push it down to even a bit quicker time. There really is no limit to what you can do when you practice.

7 Yards

Seven yards is a bit closer than the standard ten yards. At this distance, you will probably get more of a sense of some "out of control" speed. I like to pay particular attention to the draw and reload speed at this distance. Getting a turning draw down to around one second requires a really aggressive turn.

10 Yards

This is the standard distance for this drill, and I rarely shoot it at other distances.

Personally, I love driving the time down on this, and love seeing how aggressive I can be.

There are two really important times on this drill: the draw time and the reload time.

The draw time doesn't really come down to how fast you can turn; it is how fast you can get the gun up to the target. I prefer to throw my weight around and get my head looking to the first target as soon as I can. Once you have your eyes on the target, just drive the sights to it. Pay very close attention during your practice to make sure you don't pull the gun from the holster early. You really don't want to end up getting DQed in a match situation.

The other big issue is the reload. It is very common for misses to occur on the shot before you reload, and the shot you fire just after the reload. This is almost always due to rushing. Trying to race the clock is going to give you some pretty negative consequences, I would advise you to be extra sure to see your sights clearly on the shots before and after you reload.

Another common trouble spot to watch is the middle target. If you are experienced at the "Blake Drill" earlier in this section, you know it is common to "drag" shots through the targets, especially on the middle target. Make sure you stop your gun in the middle, and get two center hits.

One thing that really helps me is to shoot this drill with a target focus. I see my sights on the target, but they are blurry. Then, I drive the gun around with my eyes, and run the gun as hard as I can. Try looking *through* your gun on this drill.

Since this is such a milestone drill, I like to run it a few different ways:

Cold. Shoot this at the beginning of the practice session. Score by hit factor.

Hit Factor. Try to get the highest possible hit factor. (11-12 is pretty good for Production shooters, over 14 is heroic.)

All "A"s. Your score is your time, but you must have all "A"s. To do this consistently usually means backing way off. If you can consistently shoot **all** "A"s in the six to-seven second range, you are doing great.

Shoot for Speed. Sometimes, just for fun, I like to shoot as fast as I can. If you get 12 hits on brown, you are good to go. Your score is your time. This is such a fun exercise, but it does use a lot of ammo. I usually save it for the end

of a practice session. The real hot dogs can get well into the three-second range on this one.

15 Yards

At 15 yards, it isn't quite the "balls to the wall" hosefest that the closer distances can be. I like to let the sights settle down just a little bit more. I can't run the 15 yard distance quite as fast as I can pull the trigger, but it is awful close.

25 Yards

At 25 yards, I really focus on getting a nice stable turn (as opposed to a solely fast turn). You want to bring the gun onto target, and have the sights appear to be nice and stable. Any misalignment in your sight picture will show up in your hits.

Double, Reload, Double (Four Aces)

"Four Aces" is one of those exercises that gives you a good idea of what you can do in terms of draw speed and reload speed. The procedure is to draw and fire two rounds into the "A" zone, then reload, then fire two more rounds. I would pay particular attention to your times at the 7-and 10-yard distances. You will see those distances often on classifier stages.

3 Yards

From really close range like this, you scarcely need to aim. The primary issue here is staying relaxed, and then just "letting it happen." If you rush at all, you are prone to fumble, and it is game over at that point. I selected 2.2 seconds as a goal time for this distance.

Make absolutely no mistake, that is a seriously challenging time to make, and it will take many hours of dryfire training before you have a prayer of manipulating your gun that fast.

5 Yards

I selected 2.3 seconds as a goal time for this distance. You are still essentially going to shoot without getting a "hard" sight focus. You don't have any time to waste if you are going to make the goal time.

7 Yards

At the standard distance of seven yards, I have selected a 2.5 second goal time. This allows for a 1-second draw, a 1.1-second reload, and two 0.2-second splits. If you find yourself unable to make that 2.5-second goal time, carefully go through the data from the timer and find the "low hanging fruit."

Now, I feel like I should point out that some people can go *much* faster than the 2.5-second goal time. It is possible to get a draw time into the 0.60s, and a reload time into the 0.70s (I have heard some reported times even faster than that). The sky is absolutely the limit on this drill.

In order to be competitive in the sport, you don't need some insane reload time like a 0.75, but you do need to be able to reload the gun in about 1 second flat on a fairly consistent basis in practice. If you can't do it, then you are going to have a problem.

The key to this drill is dryfire training. This is just a "check" for you to make sure you are headed in the right direction.

10 Yards

Letting the sights settle that extra little bit is all you need to do to get "A"s at this distance. I have a goal time of 2.7 seconds. I think that time is extremely reasonable, but you don't have any time to screw around, either.

15 Yards

At 15 yards, the issue is less about the speed you go and more about being accurate. The nature of this drill means that you never really get to develop a rhythm to your shooting. This is because you are constantly fighting to get a grip on the draw, or to reacquire your grip on the reload. As I move farther and farther back, I am more concerned with getting that grip just right.

25 Yards

At 25 yards, I set a very challenging goal time of 4 seconds. This goal time requires that you draw and reload at your maximum speed, and don't "sit on" your nice clean 25-yard sight picture at all. There is no time to mess around at all, so as soon as I get a clean sight picture; it is time to start shooting.

Strong Hand Only (SHO)

This drill is just what it sounds like. The procedure is to draw the pistol and engage each target with two rounds using only your strong hand. Obviously, this is good practice for the occasional strong-hand-only shooting challenge. Some of the time limits may seem a little bit stiff for this, but don't worry. You can shoot surprisingly fast with only one hand so long as you grip the pistol very firmly.

3 Yards

It is almost freaky how fast you can shoot at close range. Personally, I am able to run my pistol as fast as I can pull the trigger and still hold the pistol in the "A" zone. For this reason, I selected two seconds as a goal time.

Make no mistake, there is no time to mess around. You are probably going to have to fire based on "index" alone, with no time for a nice crisp sight picture.

Another thing I should point out is that when you are swinging the gun between targets really aggressively, it can be difficult to precisely stop the gun in a particular place. There really isn't a good way around this difficulty. You just need to be aware not to overswing the gun.

5 Yards

I selected 2.5 seconds for the goal time at this range. For me, this range requires something of a sight picture, but not a very stable or refined picture. Again, you may be surprised just how fast you can go at this distance.

7 Yards

At seven yards, I start to worry about trigger control. I do use a DA/SA pistol, and that does make that first shot difficult. I bear down on my grip and *work* that trigger straight back. Three seconds is the goal time at this distance. This isn't a blazing time; it is just about working that trigger back without disturbing the sights at all. If you see your sights dip out of the front notch, you will likely not get an "A."

10 Yards

Shooting 10 yards strong hand only is about as difficult for me, from a marksmanship perspective, as 20-yard freestyle shooting. I treat it accordingly. I let the sights come down and settle down a bit before pressing the trigger straight back again. The goal time of 3.5 seconds leaves plenty of time for this.

15 Yards

Shooting at 15 yards strong hand only is obviously pretty unusual in a match situation, but it does occasionally happen. In any event, working at this distance, or further, will give you a good deal of confidence to know that you can handle anything closer.

25 Yards

The six-second goal time at 25 yards is something I feel is very reasonable. You will have time to let the sight return, and to get a smooth trigger break. There is no reason to rush at this distance.

If you are one of those people that prefers to tilt the gun slightly when you shoot one-handed, then you may see a noticeable point of impact shift when you shoot from this far back. I realize that it is perhaps a bit more comfortable to give your gun that "gangsta" tilt, but if you need to make tight or long shots one-handed, you will see that your sights don't work properly when you tilt them. This is certainly an issue you need to consider.

50 Yards

I included this distance as a challenge for you. I think it is fun to push the limits of what you can do. The goal time is 10 seconds. That is certainly a significant amount of time under normal circumstances, but you will use it up quickly on this drill. With a DA/SA pistol, it is very difficult to get an "A" on the first shot when you are working the double action trigger throw. In any event, I enjoy the challenge, and I encourage you to try it. If you can get all six rounds onto the cardboard, you are a stud in my book.

Weak Hand Only (WHO)

The procedure for "Weak Hand Only" is to draw and transfer the gun to your weak hand, and then engage each target with two rounds. Now, many shooters rarely, if ever, practice weak hand only shooting. I can assure you that a bit of practice on this will increase your confidence level on weak-handed shooting generally, and will also help you learn about good trigger control. Weak-hand shooting in matches tends to be a rare event, and to be honest, it isn't that much fun, but there is no reason for you to fall behind your competitors.

3 Yards

When working from this close, it is almost freaky how fast you can go. It feels weird to me to run my gun this hard weak hand only, but it is certainly something you should try. You frequently see weak-hand shooting at close range. You need to know how fast you can go!

I picked a three-second goal time for this distance. About half of that will be just for the draw and transfer to weak hand. If you don't dryfire weak-handed shooting regularly, you may have problems making this par time.

7 Yards

At seven yards, you shouldn't have too hard of a time punching "A"s. I like to remind myself that sight alignment isn't really all that important at this close of a range. If you are sending shots really far off target, it is almost always going to be due to your trigger control. People have a strong tendency to tense up their firing hand to try and control recoil, and it causes problems in a major way. I call this "firing the gun with your whole hand." Be warned, this problem doesn't usually manifest itself during slow fire, but when you try to make a tight time limit, it becomes a problem.

15 Yards

In a match situation, 15 yards is about as far away as I can recall shooting weak-handed. I don't worry too much about being quick. If you are looking to shave time off, I would work on the draw and transfer to your weak hand. It is difficult to really ramp up the shooting speed.

25 Yards

This distance is tough. I doubt you will ever see shots this far in a match that you are required to take weak-hand only, but you should certainly try it as a skill builder.

50 Yards

For a match situation, 50 yards is obviously ridiculous, but I think it is fun and something you should certainly try if you are so inclined. I think challenging yourself to the point where things are so difficult as to be comical is a great way to end a day on the range and a great way to learn. You never know, you might surprise yourself and get some "A"s.

Bill/Reload

The Bill/Reload drill is a fun little test of trigger speed and relaxation at close distances, and pretty much a rehash of the "Bill Drill" at longer ranges. This drill eats up ammunition in a hurry, but if you have the bullets to spare, I recommend you give this one a go.

The procedure for this drill is to draw, engage a single target with six rounds, execute a reload, and reengage the target with an additional six rounds.

I like to take a close look at all of my split times on the timer when working this drill. By the time you get into this drill, you should have a good idea of draw times, reload times, and "Bill Drill" times at any given distance. In theory, your times shouldn't change. In practice, you will tend to run slower on any given task when you string a bunch of tasks together. I like to keep that in mind when running this drill.

3 Yards

The three-yards distance is very similar to the famous USPSA classifier stage "Can You Count."

At this distance, your biggest enemy is likely going to be tensing up as you go for a fast time. I picked a goal time of four seconds for this distance. That is 12 rounds fired out of your pistol, a draw, and a reload at absolutely breakneck pace.

The problem at extreme close range like this usually turns out to be the reload. When people are going crazy, shedding lead as fast as they can pull the trigger, it causes their hands and forearms to get tense. It is tough to then go from tensed down on the pistol to relaxed hands that can dexterously grab the next mag, and stuff it into the gun. I take deep, relaxing breaths when I am on the line practicing this one. I shake out my hands to battle the tension. This one can get you worked up even when you are on the range by yourself. With an audience (like at a match), it is even tougher.

In any event, if you are able to stuff a reload in under a second, you are doing well on this drill. First-shot times in the 0.80s are acceptable.

7 Yards

At seven yards, you should be shooting about as fast as you are at three yards. The difference is it takes just a hair longer to get on target

Ben performing "Bill/Reload"

after the draw and the reload. As soon as you are on target with your grip, and built it up effectively, you should be able to rock and roll at maximum trigger speed.

10 Yards

At 10 yards, you will almost certainly need to back off some from your top speed trigger press, or you will see your group open up considerably. I usually stick with shooting target focused, but I make sure the front sight is back down in the notch before breaking the next shot.

25 Yards

From the 25-yard line, there really isn't much you can do to shoot superfast. What you should be doing is making sure you nail the grip when you draw and reload. I like to feel for an index point on the gun for each of those things. If you hit your index point on the gun (getting your thumb in a specific spot, or some other index point), then you really increase your chance of hitting a good grip. Once the grip is good, simply execute the fundamental mechanics.

The Heads

Head boxes are a fact of life in USPSA, and I think it makes good sense to practice for them. The procedure for this drill is to draw and engage each head box with two rounds.

Now, if you have spent any amount of time shooting USPSA, you have certainly encountered head shots. This drill should prepare you.

Due to the unique shape of head boxes, I score this drill differently based on the

distance. I will note at each distance what the scoring standard is. At close ranges, we are looking for all "A"s. At longer ranges, it becomes increasingly acceptable to get "B"s. At 25 yards, getting two hits anywhere in the head is acceptable.

The primary challenge is the extremely small "A" box in the head of the targets. It is so challenging to hit at long distance that it doesn't really make sense in the USPSA scoring system to accept only "A"s. However, as hard as the "A" zone is to hit at longer range, at close range it is extremely doable. Shooters tend to slop hits on the head box at close range because it seems like too much work to go for "A"s. This drill should help you learn to correct these problems.

5 Yards

At five yards, you should be able to hit all "A"s. This requires bringing the gun to a complete stop for every shot and getting a clear sight picture, but all "A"s is certainly appropriate.

I find that it is very helpful to know *exactly* where bullets strike the target in relation to my sights. Does the bullet hit on top of the front sight blade? On top of the fiber dot? Depending on how your gun is set up, you may need to aim at the top edge or the bottom edge of the "A" zone in order to hit it. If you are shooting an Open gun with a red dot, you may be aiming at the top edge of the head in order to get "A" hits. You need to remember the appropriate aiming point and be comfortable executing it. There is no reason to be giving away points on head shots if you can just pick the right spot in the first place.

15 Yards

I strongly feel that you can still hit "A"s with some regularity at 15 yards. I don't beat myself up for dropping "B"s, though. You may have a tendency to loosen up your grip due to the shots being a bit tougher; I urge you not to do that. It usually leads to not returning the gun back down to the target after a shot is fired, and then your follow-up shot will go high.

25 Yards

Hitting the head anywhere at 25 yards is extremely challenging, let along hitting the "A" box. I have a generous goal time of six seconds set to allow ample time for a good sight picture on every shot. Be sure to use that time.

Crisscross

The Crisscross is a distance change, or "gear change," drill. The procedure is as follows:

Draw and engage the head of one target with two rounds, the body of the middle target with two rounds, and the head of the final target with two rounds. Reload and engage the body of one target with two rounds, the head of the middle target with two rounds, then the body of the final target with two rounds. At the end of the drill, you should have engaged each body and each head, firing a total of 12 rounds. If you wish, you may shoot the reverse engagement order (body, head, body, reload, head, body, head).

This is the most complicated drill that I have included in the standard exercises section. You have constant "gear" changes, and lots of gun handling.

I think you should score this one using hit factor, essentially meaning that you are going to drop a few points in order to put up a really fast time. Usually the dropped points are going to be in the head box, but not always.

5 Yards

Even at just five yards, you should have some respect for the head shots. They may be close, but it is far too easy to send an errant shot over the head when you are really trying to rail on it. On the other hand, the lower "A" zone shots are fair game for you to go at using your top trigger speed. It isn't easy.

10 Yards

I imagine that 10 yards would be the standard distance for this drill. The shot difficulty is a pretty good analog for what you would commonly encounter in classifiers and other "stand and shoot" tests. This distance doesn't have the extreme speed of the closer distances, nor the hair pulling frustration of the longer distances. You simply cruise through and make sure you nail down a good draw and a good reload.

20 Yards

The head shots are *tough* at 20 yards; there is no doubt about it. I love having the mix of needing to execute a fairly complicated engagement order, fast gun handling, and mid-range shooting with the extremely challenging head shots. You need to bring just enough control to those head boxes to make sure you hit them, but then get back on the gas. This is an extremely challenging exercise! I wouldn't mess around with this until you can consistently make 20-yard head shots at speed. You may unnecessarily frustrate yourself if you throw so many elements in play at once without even being able to make the shots to begin with.

Standard Exercise Quick Reference Goal Times

I thought it would be beneficial to consolidate the goal times for the "Standard Practice Setup." This may be a good thing for you to keep in your range bag, or to refer to before you head out to shoot.

Please note, if you see an NA on the chart, it means that I didn't list a goal time for that distance. This is because either the drill doesn't make sense to shoot at that distance, or I thought that the distance was repetitious in some way.

Obviously there are other drills that you could be running on the standard setup.

Essentially, the sky is the limit. I simply outlined a few of the more common drills, and gave appropriate times and commentary. The point I want to make is that based on the data already included in this book, you should be able to infer appropriate goal times for any other drill you wish to run.

For example, you could shoot each target with one round, then reload and shoot each target with one more round. This is the same thing as running "Singles," reloading, and running it again. Since draw times and reload times tend to be broadly similar, you should know that by doubling the goal time (at any given distance) for "Singles," you would have a pretty good benchmark for what you would be running this new drill in (Let's call it "Singles/Reload/Singles").

Be creative! After you get tired of running these drills, come up with some other drills and run them instead.

Distance	3 yards	5 yards	7 yards	10 yards	15 yards	20 yards	25 yards	50 yards
Doubles	1.0	1.1	1.2	1.3	1.5	1.8	2.0	3.0
Bill Drill	1.7	1.8	2.0	2.2	2.5	3.2	4.0	6.0
Blake Drill	NA	1.8	2.0	2.2	2.5	NA	NA	NA
Singles	1.2	1.3	1.4	1.6	1.8	2.2	2.6	NA
El Prez	NA	NA	4.8	5.0	6.0	7.0	8.0	12
Four Aces	2.2	2.3	2.5	2.7	3.0	3.5	4.0	6.0
SHO	2.0	2.5	3.0	3.5	4.0	5.0	6.0	10
WHO	3.0	3.5	4.0	4.5	5.0	6.0	8.0	12
Bill/Reload	4.0	4.2	4.5	5.0	6.0	7.0	7.5	12
Heads	NA	3.0	3.5	4.0	5.0	5.5	6.0	NA
Crisscross	NA	5.0	5.5	6.0	7.0	8.0	NA	NA

Wide Setup

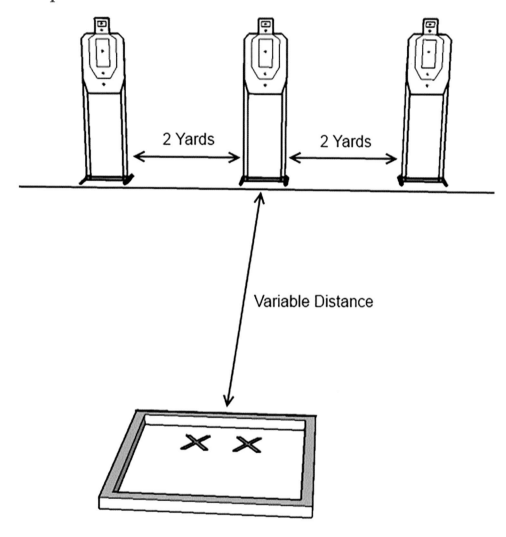

Date:	Par Time:	Notes:
	NA	
	NA	
	NA	
	NA	
	NA	
	NA	
	NA	
	NA	
	NA	
	NA	

The "Wide Setup" is essentially the same thing as the "Standard Practice Setup." By extending the distance between targets, you can really emphasize your target transition skills. To be honest, the "Standard Practice Setup" usually only requires you to push your gun over a bit, and you are on the next target. By increasing the transition distance, you really need to hunt for the center of the "A" zone with your eyes.

I have included goal times for all the applicable drills. Obviously, the drills shot on a single target are omitted from this list, because no target transitioning is involved in those drills, and it wouldn't make sense to include them again.

All the drill procedures and commentary from the standard setup still apply; I simply worked in some longer times to account for the increased target transition distance.

I didn't extend this list out past 20 yards, because once the distance is extended that much, there isn't that much of an effect on the times.

Distance	3 yards	5 yards	7 yards	10 yards	15 yards	20 yards
Blake Drill	NA	2.0	2.2	2.4	2.7	NA
Singles	1.4	1.5	1.6	1.8	2.0	2.4
El Prez	NA	NA	5.2	5.4	6.4	NA
SHO	2.2	2.7	3.2	3.7	4.2	5.2
WHO	3.2	3.7	4.2	4.7	5.2	6.2
Heads	NA	3.2	3.7	4.2	5.2	NA
Crisscross	NA	6.5	7.0	7.5	8.5	9.5

Super Wide Setup

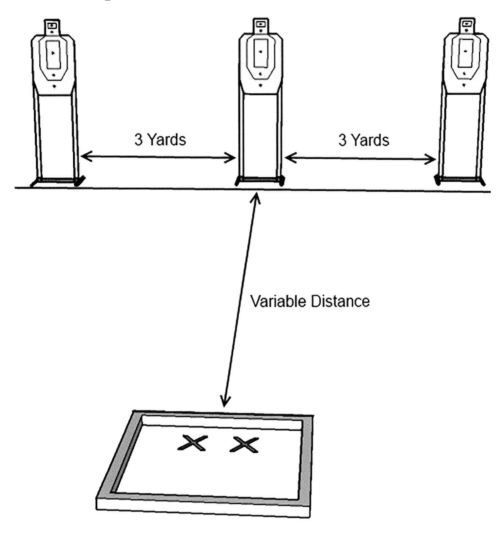

Date:	Par Time:	Notes:
	NA	
	NA	
	NA	
	NA	
	NA	
	NA	
	NA	
	NA	
	NA	
	NA	

The "Super Wide Setup" is essentially the same thing as the "Standard Practice Setup." By extending the distance between targets, you can emphasize your target transition skills. To be honest, the "Standard Practice Setup" usually just requires you to push your gun over a bit, and you are then on the next target. By tripling the transition distance from the standard setup, you will need to hunt for the "A" zone visually, and muscle the gun to the next target.

Some of the closer-range drills are extremely challenging to go fast on with so much distance between the targets. You may have a sensation of "muscling" the gun around.

I have included goal times for all the applicable drills. Obviously, the drills shot on a single target are omitted from this list, because no target transitioning is involved.

All the drill procedures and commentary from the standard setup still apply, but I worked in some longer times to account for the increased target transition distance.

I didn't extend this list out past 20 yards, because once the distance is extended that much, there isn't that much of an effect on the times.

Distance	3 yards	5 yards	7 yards	10 yards	15 yards	20 yards
Blake Drill	NA	2.2	2.4	2.6	2.8	NA
Singles	1.6	1.7	1.8	2.0	2.2	2.6
El Prez	NA	NA	5.6	5.8	6.8	NA
SHO	2.4	2.9	3.4	3.9	4.4	5.4
WHO	3.4	3.9	4.4	5.9	5.4	6.4
Heads	NA	3.4	3.9	4.4	5.4	NA
Crisscross	NA	7.0	7.5	8.0	9.0	10

Six-Target Setup

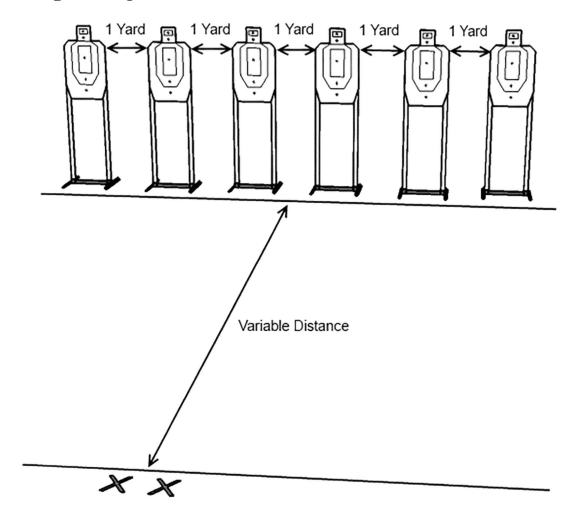

Date:	Par Time:	Notes:
	NA	
	NA	
	NA	
	NA	
	NA	
	NA	
	NA	
	NA	
	NA	
	NA	

You may want to try single shots on a target as opposed to always shooting two rounds at everything. If that is the case, you can use the "Six-Target Setup" that I have here. Each target is engaged with only one round, as opposed to two rounds. For example, during a "Blake Drill," you would still fire six rounds. One round goes into each target, as opposed to two rounds going into each of three targets. I have again provided a chart with goal times for the applicable drills at each distance.

Distance	3 yards	5 yards	7 yards	10 yards	15 yards	20 yards
Blake Drill	NA	2.5	2.7	2.8	3.0	3.5
El Prez	NA	NA	6.0	6.5	7.0	7.5
SHO	3.0	3.5	4.0	4.5	5.0	5.5
WHO	3.5	4.0	4.5	5.5	6.0	7.0
Heads	NA	4.0	4.5	5.0	5.5	6.0

The Plate Rack

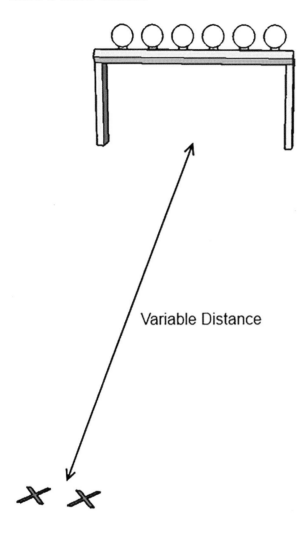

Variable Distance

Plate racks are a common toy to have hanging around shooting clubs. They come in a variety of shapes and sizes, but most of them are "Bianchi style" plate racks. That is to say, they are six plates, eight inches in diameter, arranged in a straight line.

I don't know any shooter that doesn't enjoy banging away on steel at least occasionally. Since these plate racks are so common, I have included a set of drills that you can try. Before we get to the drills, I want to make a few comments about plate racks in general.

First, I think plate racks are a good shooting skill test, and an interesting diversion from your practice. You need to shoot steel targets occasionally during your practice to get used to them. There is a "lag time" when you are shooting at steel, and it takes some getting used to. When you get going in a big hurry, you need to be transitioning to the next steel target before you hear the sound of hitting the first steel target. You will see steel falling out of the corner of your eye long after you actually shoot it. It can be distracting. You need to be trained to a point where you don't notice that stuff.

Date:	Par Time:	Notes:
	NA	
	NA	
	NA	
	NA	
	NA	
	NA	
	NA	
	NA	
	NA	
	NA	

Similarly, when you are working on steel, you need to get used to not having a "C" zone to soak up your bad shots. You will either hit the plate or you will not. If you don't, you need to fire a fast makeup shot. This is a good thing to be trained to do, because in a match situation, you need to be at the point where you don't hesitate to fire makeups if you need them.

All of this feedback you get from shooting steel can damage you. Paper targets don't let you know if you missed them, you need to call the shots off your sights. Some shooters that practice primarily on steel develop a reliance on the feedback from the steel, and it hurts them in a match situation. For that reason, I don't think you should go too heavy on plate racks. Shooting them now and then is helpful and fun, but if you feel yourself becoming reliant on the audible or visual feedback from the steel, then you should switch to paper for a while.

Straight Six

The "Straight Six" is just what it sounds like. You draw your pistol and shoot down all six of the plates. A big theme here is going to be nailing the draw. If you do that, it makes life easy when it comes to driving all the plates down.

10 Yards

At 10 yards, you should be able to put your focus on the targets, and shoot the plates down. It will speed things up, but it makes aiming more difficult. It takes most shooters a bit of work to get used to aiming with a blurry

sight picture. At least at 10 yards, you don't need very precise alignment to hit the plates. Look for a 1.1 or 1.2 draw in order to make the 2.5-second total time.

15 Yards

Interestingly enough, you don't need to back off a whole lot at 15 yards as opposed to 10 yards. I spend just a little bit more time confirming a solid grip and first shot from the draw, and then I can run just about as aggressively as I can at the closer ranges.

One thing you can certainly experiment with at 15 yards is target-focused shooting, as opposed to front sight-focused shooting. At this distance, I find the two methods to be broadly similar in terms of results. The feel of those methods (in a subjective sense) are very different. Target focused feels aggressive and rock solid. Sight focused feels like more work, but I can tell where on each plate the bullets will strike just by watching the sights. I encourage you to experiment.

25 Yards

I selected a goal time of five seconds at this distance. It is a challenging goal to hit with any regularity. I find that a 0.6 or 0.7 split is fairly normal at this distance. With every extra shot costing that much time, you really don't want to have any misses.

You may not see many 25 yard plates in matches, but you will often want to shoot with a high degree of precision. You will certainly learn to do that by mastering the plate rack at 25 yards.

Pick Two

"Pick Two" is simply drawing and shooting two adjacent plates. This is a drill I use to make sure I am nailing down a solid draw. I find that most of my problems on a plate rack are going to be related in some way to the quality of my grip and draw, so it makes sense to cut the round count down and work on just the draw.

10 Yards

At 10 yards, you may be surprised what you can get away with in terms of sight picture. I have had good success with target focus, but maybe not as much consistency as sight-focused shooting. I selected a goal time of 1.5 seconds. That time is extremely reasonable, but remember that I picked it as a consistent time. I have seen shooters draw and hit two plates in about a second, but there isn't much consistency there. See how many times in a row you can get under 1.5 seconds.

25 Yards

Fundamentally, nothing changes at 25 yards. You have a lot more time, and you should use it. Get the sharpest sight picture you can, and do not rush your shooting. You have three seconds to shoot down two plates. The challenge is going one for one, not being fast.

Three Load Three

"Three Load Three" is a gun handling exercise you can do with your plate rack. You draw, take three plates, reload, then take three more plates. I find that on this drill, I spend most of the time doing the gun handling. To be clear,

less than half of the total time is going to be actually firing the shots.

10 Yards

This is a good distance to pay extra close attention to the times. This is your standard distance for many of the classifiers, and an eight inch plate is slightly tougher than an "A" zone. I find I can add about 0.2 seconds on to my normal draw and reload times at this distance by shooting at a plate instead of a cardboard target.

25 Yards

Obviously, 25 yards is going to be the most challenging distance from a marksmanship perspective. I get frustrated at this distance sometimes. If you shoot plates at 25 yards, you know that getting your grip perfect is challenging. It is hard to get your sights tracking right for you. When things are clicking, you can smash the plates down with little effort. When I draw the gun, get my grip right, and start shooting, the last thing I want to do is break grip for a reload. It is tough to get into a rhythm on this drill, and that makes it good practice.

Strong Hand Only (SHO)

"Strong Hand Only" is just what it sounds like. You draw and shoot all the plates with your dominant hand only. I have set times that I feel are realistic on this. At 10 yards, 3.5 seconds is quick, but reasonable. You get eight seconds at 25 yards, though it really isn't as much time as it sounds like. You have a chance at every distance to take the time to confirm sight alignment, and then press the trigger straight back. You need to be patient, but this is doable.

I don't believe that you will see a whole lot of this sort of thing in a match, but it is a great skill builder.

Weak Hand Only (WHO)

"Weak Hand Only" is just like "Strong Hand Only," except the time limits take the transfer to your weak hand into account. Also, I allow for more time as they get long and longer. This drill is particularly challenging for people shooing DA/SA guns, as they will need to nail plates with a double action trigger.

Just like with "Strong Hand Only," I don't believe that you will see a whole lot of this sort of thing in a match, but it is a fantastic skill builder.

Classifiers

I think if you really want to understand how to shoot classifiers effectively, you should set up and practice on some classifiers. Before I get too deep into this, I want to be clear on a few points.

First, as I pointed out earlier in the book, I am not focused on teaching people to "make GM." I want you to *be a GM*. Of course, there are a few different training methods that will get you there, but in my opinion, a GM should be able to shoot quickly and accurately, handle the gun efficiently and consistently, and understand the scoring system to the level where they don't need to pull out a calculator to have a good idea of where they stand.

I know there are some ethical objections from some people when it comes to practicing classifiers. Objections range from getting a

Distance	10 yards	15 yards	20 yards	25 yards
Single Six	2.5	3.0	4.0	5.0
Pick Two	1.5	2.0	2.5	3.0
SHO	3.5	5.0	6.5	8.0
WHO	4.5	6.5	8.5	10
Three Load Three	4.0	5.0	6.0	7.0

classification you can't be competitive in, to the idea that it is unethical to practice for "the test."

Let me just say, I practice classifier stages extensively. I don't do this in order to move up in terms of classification (I already am a GM). I do this because they give me the ability to take a stage that I have quite a bit of information about, and work on it. Earlier in this section, I outlined a number of drills, and gave you a good deal of data about those

drills. Many shooters have found that data to be absolutely invaluable information. It helps shape your practice and direct your efforts to areas where you can make the largest gains in your score for the least amount of effort. Classifiers are helpful this way. You have a stage with a data set to go along with it. I think it is foolish in the extreme not to utilize the information available about classifiers to improve your own shooting.

Another important thing about practicing classifier stages is that it is a super easy way to learn the scoring system in the level of detail that you need to know it. Instead of working for a goal time, you are going to work for a hit factor. This means you will need to calculate hit factors while you are on the range. After getting comfortable with this process, you will have a much better idea of how the scoring system works, and how to maximize your own score.

The Process

Through my own training and development, I settled on a logical system for using classifiers to train. I think using this process is very helpful, and it makes for an excellent practice session. You will learn a lot about your own abilities. You can learn where to direct your practice efforts, and you will learn what it takes to be a GM.

The first step of this process is to pick a classifier stage. These diagrams are available on internet forums, USPSA's website, and other places as well. I think you should pick a classifier that is simple to set up. I try to stay away from the ones that require specially constructed wall sections or some other special prop. There are enough classifiers that just require a few target stands that there isn't much of a need to set up the more complicated ones.

After selecting a classifier, you need to retrieve score data on that classifier. There are a number of ways you can go about this. First, if it is a classifier you have already shot, you should know your hit factor and the

percentage that USPSA assigned to your score. So, for example, if you shot "El Presidente" at a recent club match with a 4.7829 hit factor. When the classifier update hits the USPSA website, they assigned a national score of 46.6118 percent. From that data, you are able to calculate the High Hit Factor (HHF) for that stage. In other words, you can figure out what 100 percent is in terms of hit factor. I suppose you could figure out other benchmarks as well, but it has always seemed sensible to me to have aggressive goals.

The formula to calculate HHF is this:
(100/National Percentage) × hit factor = HHF
Plugging in the example from above:
(100/46.6118) = 2.1453
2.1453 × 4.7829 = 10.2607

So, as you can see, you can do some quick math and come up with the HHF for a classifier before you ever go to the range to shoot it. You can use data from friends or from complete strangers. It just doesn't matter. As soon as USPSA assigns a shooter a score for any classifier stage, you can figure out the HHF just by knowing the hit factor shot on the stage and the national percentage. This data is great for your own training.

Knowing the HHF isn't the end of the story as far as collecting data. The HHF assigned by USPSA is one thing, but knowing what hit factors people actually shoot on the stage is helpful as well. Again, checking around on internet forums and talking with experienced shooters can clue you in. Some classifiers have a reputation for being "easy" to do well on, while others have a reputation for being extremely difficult to get a "good" score on. There are classifiers that some of the best shooters in the world can have a "good" run on, and get back a score from USPSA of 80 percent. I am not pointing to this to criticize the classification system, just pointing out that you should try and get a picture of the specific classifier stage you are going to shoot. You may want to adjust your goal up to 115 percent, down to 85 percent, or whatever makes sense for that particular classifier. It all depends on the specifics of the stage. This is perhaps a bit more of an art than a science, but it is something you should be aware of.

I think it is helpful to make some predictions before you head out to the range. What I mean is that you should get an idea of how a 100 percent classifier run will break down. I will continue on with the "El Presidente" example (If you don't recall the procedure for "El Presidente," it is outlined earlier in this section).

What I mean by this is that you should try to figure out a realistic way to get a 100 percent score. So, if you were to shoot 60 points (all "A"s) in 5.84 seconds, it would work out to a 100 percent run. Similarly, if you shoot 46 points (five "A"s and seven "C"s scoring minor) in 4.48 seconds, you will score the same 100 percent run. If you are eyeballing those numbers, and one seems really quick, but inaccurate, and the other seems a bit slow, but very accurate, then you are right. I don't think it is a realistic to plan to shoot all "A"s on a classifier, nor do I think it is productive to shoot at an out of control pace. For the drill

"El Presidente," the goal time is five seconds. This is because experience has taught me that the way to get 100 percent runs on stages consistently is to go a hair slower than top speed. You run right on the edge. Shooting at a pace to guarantee all "A"s every time is a recipe for bad scores.

In any event, as you get some experience working through classifiers and training on the "Standard Practice Setup," you will be able to eyeball times that are appropriate. I will go through this process in some detail for the four example classifiers that I have included in this book. Just as a tip, I think it is rare that you should be estimating a run where you are going to shoot all "A"s on a classifier. It doesn't happen that often, and aside from a few outlier classifiers (at extreme close range), you should plan on dropping some points.

When you get to the range, set up the classifier as close to the specified diagram as you possibly can. If you don't have the tools to measure out distances with precision, I recommend you err on the side of difficulty. Set the targets a bit farther away than needed in order to ensure they are far enough away. Set them a bit farther apart than necessary for the same reason.

After setup, I prefer to run the classifier once, cold. I prepare myself mentally and physically the same way I would in a match. The idea is to produce a bit of match pressure. Your first run on a classifier stage (even though it is in practice) should be meaningful. Think about it. You know what a "good" score is. You have a goal. You know what you are trying to do. Either you are going to be successful, or you are going to fail; it is as simple as that. If you are serious about training and development, then you should be mentally and emotionally invested in your shooting. It doesn't matter that you aren't testing yourself at a match; you are testing yourself all the same.

After shooting the classifier cold, I make a point of carefully calculating my hit factor. Of course, with a bit of experience, you should be able to make rough calculations in your head. When you are just learning the scoring system, however, you may need to use a calculator. As you should know, hit factor is simply points divided by time.

The way I calculate hit factor quickly is to subtract the points dropped on the stage from the points available, and then divide by the time. For example, if I shoot "El Prez" in 5.29 seconds with a total of eight "A"s, two "C"s, one "D," and one miss, then the math works like this: There is a maximum of 60 points available on this stage. I start by deducting from that number. Two "C"s is 4 points. One "D" is 4 points. One miss is 15 points. Together, that is 23 points subtracted from the maximum of 60 points. That is 37 points divided by 5.29 seconds for a hit factor of 6.99. Obviously, that is a poor run. If anything, you will find that the math is a lot easier as you drop fewer points (the above example was calculated using minor scoring).

After you shoot the classifier the first time, take a careful look at the timer. What was your draw time? What was your reload time (if there was one)? What about your split times? You should carefully go through the

information on the timer. If you are working through the exercises in this section, you should have a very good idea of what sort of times you can lay down for just about any action at any distance.

If you are "off" when you are running a classifier stage cold, then welcome to the club. Virtually everyone is going to be a hair slower for the first run of the day than they are during practice. The idea is to build consistency with your training. **Paying attention to the first run of the day will give you a lot of insight into the overall effectiveness of your training.**

After you shoot the whole stage a few times, it is helpful to break that stage into smaller drills. You can come up with your own goal times for these drills based on the information you already have. For example, if I was going to work on the "El Presidente" as a series of drills, I would try the following set of drills:

- Turning, drawing, and engaging one target with two rounds (goal time 1.4)
- "Four Aces" (goal time 2.7)
- "Blake Drill" (goal time 2.2)

Distance for all drills is 10 yards.

If those drills and times look familiar, then that is a good thing. All of those drills were pulled from the "Standard Practice Setup" earlier in this section. The exception to this was the turn and draw drill, which was the same thing as the "Doubles" drill, but I added a tenth of a second to allow for turning around during the draw. If you work through the drills in this section, you will quickly and easily be able to identify the individual parts of the larger classifier stage that you can work on. I also included a set of "micro drills" for you to play around with on each classifier.

After working through these smaller drills, I like to make a mental note (and later a paper note) of the areas I think I may want to focus some practice on later. Perhaps I need to clean up my reload, my transitions, or whatever. By taking a close look at the split times, not just the aggregate time, you are going to get a lot of important information about what you can improve.

At the end of the day, there is a lot to be learned by working through this process. I literally have done this for almost every classifier in the USPSA book. I learned a lot.

A Few of the Key Lessons

The best hit factors are going to come from shooting all "A"s.

The key times to focus on are draw times and reload times. They have a big effect on the overall classifier time.

Most A class shooters pull the trigger at roughly the same speed as GMs. The difference is in the draw, reloads, and target transitions.

There isn't time to get a nice clean sight picture for every shot. Shooting a classifier well means that you are right on the edge of shooting out of control.

At the end of the day, reading this stuff in a book isn't going to make you a good shooter. You need to get out to the range and experiment for yourself. You need to learn the nuances of the classification system and the scoring system. I picked out a few sample classifier stages to run through this process. I feel these classifiers are representative of the larger system. If you master them, you will be in a good position to do well on any other classifier stage that you encounter.

Front Sight

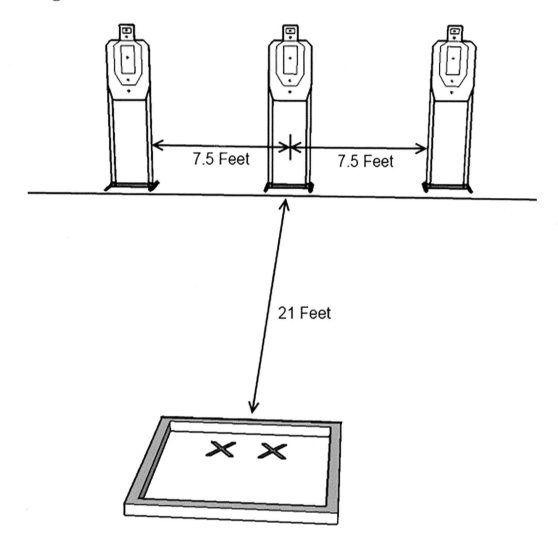

Date:	Par Time:	Notes:
	NA	
	NA	
	NA	
	NA	
	NA	
	NA	
	NA	
	NA	
	NA	
	NA	

Setup Notes:
Set the targets five feet high at the shoulders. The box is three feet by three feet.

Procedure:
Standing in box, both arms hanging relaxed at sides or both wrists above respective shoulders (shooter's choice).

- String 1: Start facing uprange. Upon start signal, turn, from Box A engage T1-T3 with only two rounds per target.
- String 2: Start facing targets, hand position opposite of string one, upon start signal, from Box A, engage T1-T3 with only two rounds per target.

Focus:
This classifier emphasizes fast transitioning on close targets.

Goal:
Try to shoot 10 percent above your current classification.

Commentary:
Front Sight is one of those classifiers that is a lot tougher than it looks. The targets are all close, sure, but the high hit factor is so stout that you are going to need to be driving the gun around hard and precisely in order to stand a chance of getting a good score. Remember, anyone can shoot this stage and walk away feeling like they went fast and shot mostly "A"s. Your goal is to be able to consistently shoot good enough for a 100 percent score.

First, you do have a choice in this classifier to decide your hand position for each string. I recommend you go with wrists above your shoulders for the string you need to turn and draw on, and hands at sides for the string where you don't turn. I don't think there is much of a time difference here, but you probably will be more conversant with the turning draw from a wrists above shoulders position.

Again, the hit factor on this one is high enough that you don't have any time to screw around. The time for each string needs to average about two seconds total! That means you need to hit that one second draw in order to have a chance.

For me, the key challenge here has always been making sure my gun stops in the center of each target. If you move the gun to the wrong spot, you drop points and damage your score. If you shoot as you move the gun, you drag your hits on and off the target, maybe even scoring a miss. This classifier tests your transitions like no other.

Suggested Micro Drills:
Turn, draw, and engage *one* target with only two rounds.

Turn, draw, and engage *each* target with only one round.

Draw and engage *one* target with two rounds.

Engage *each* target with one round.

High Standards

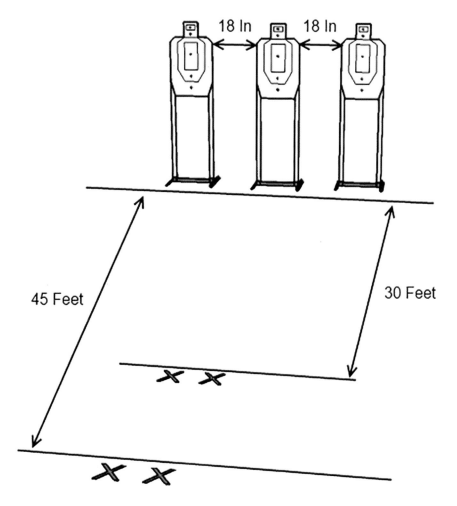

Date:	Par Time:	Notes:
	NA	
	NA	
	NA	
	NA	
	NA	
	NA	
	NA	
	NA	
	NA	
	NA	

Setup Notes:
Set the targets five feet high at the shoulders.

Procedure:
Start with your hands relaxed at sides for both strings.

- String 1: From behind the 15-yard fault line, engage each target with only two rounds. Perform a mandatory reload and re-engage each target with only two more rounds, **strong hand only.**
- String 2: From behind the 10-yard fault line, engage each target with only two rounds. Perform a mandatory reload, and re-engage each target with only two more rounds, **weak hand only.**

Focus:
This classifier is a good test of both gun handling and single-handed shooting skills.

Goal:
Try to shoot 10 percent above your current classification.

Commentary:
This classifier is fun because there are a few different elements involved. The gun handling is intense. You have two draws, two reloads, and a transfer to your weak hand. There is no time to mess around with any of this stuff. There, of course, is some single-handed shooting. There is also some freestyle shooting at mid-range.

I think the best part about this classifier is that there really is nothing hard about it, but you need to be proficient with that whole broad base of skills. If you aren't able to get the high hit factor, then take a look at all of your split times to figure out where you need to pick the time up. Make sure you are being accurate on every string.

When you are shooting with only one hand, trigger control is going to be much more difficult. I find my hand tensing up to control the recoil, and it makes it difficult to move the trigger finger independently. I always feel "on the edge" during the single hand portions of this classifier because I need to shoot just a bit faster than I am comfortable in order to nail that high hit factor.

Suggested Micro Drills:
From the 15-yard line, engage each target with two rounds.

From the 15-yard line, engage each target with two rounds, strong hand only.

From the 10-yard line, engage each target with two rounds.

From the 10-yard line, engage each target with two rounds, weak hand only.

Quicky II

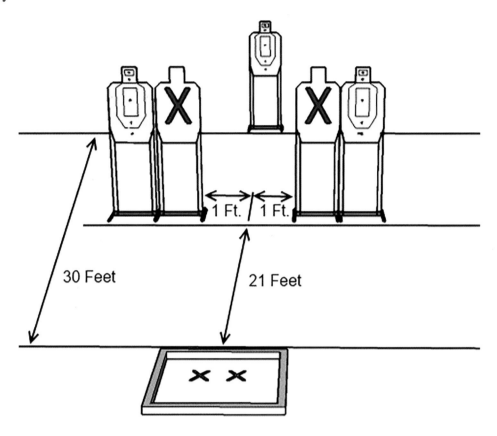

30 Feet

21 Feet

1 Ft. / 1 Ft.

Date:	Par Time:	Notes:
	NA	
	NA	
	NA	
	NA	
	NA	
	NA	
	NA	
	NA	
	NA	
	NA	

Setup Notes:

When setting up this classifier, don't be confused about the no-shoot targets. They are positioned in such a way that it is fair to consider them a non-issue. I usually omit them from setup for this reason.

Procedure:

The start position for both strings is reaching overhead for a box, arms extended, elbows locked.

- String 1: Upon start signal, from Box A engage T1-T3 with only two rounds per target, then make a mandatory reload, and from Box A engage T1-T3 with only two rounds per target using strong hand only.

- String 2: Upon start signal, from Box A engage T1-T3 with only two rounds per target, then make a mandatory reload, and from Box A engage T1-T3 with only two rounds per target using weak hand only.

Jams may be cleared with both hands.

Focus:

This classifier is a good test of both gun handling and single-handed shooting skills.

Goal:

Try to shoot 10 percent above your current classification.

Commentary:

This classifier essentially has the same challenges as High Standards, but it is closer and even faster. I have seen string times well under five seconds on this for the first string, and just over five seconds for the second string. You will be amazed at just how fast you can go!

The challenging thing for me here is to shoot target focused even when only one hand is on the gun. It is hard to do!

Suggested Micro Drills:

Engage each target with two rounds.

Engage each target with two rounds, strong hand only.

Engage each target with two rounds, weak hand only.

Tight Squeeze

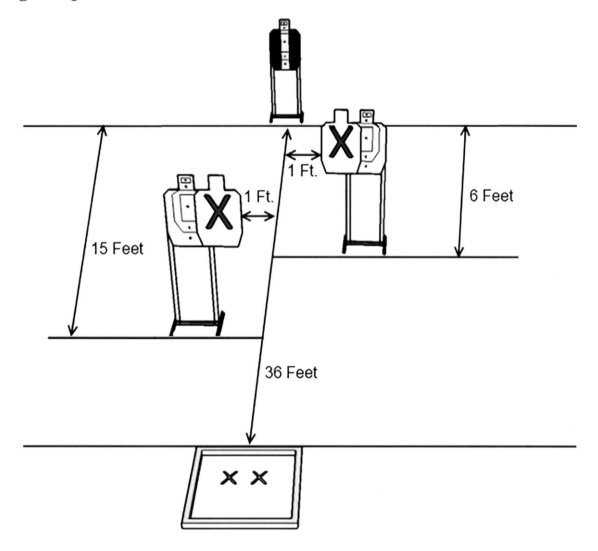

Date:	Par Time:	Notes:
	NA	
	NA	
	NA	
	NA	
	NA	
	NA	
	NA	
	NA	
	NA	
	NA	

Setup Notes:

Set paper targets five feet high at the shoulders. Hard cover on the back target is even with the edge of the "A" zone. The no-shoots on the other targets are placed so the perforation of the edge of the no-shoot is even with the "A" zone of the shoot target.

Procedure:

Engage each target with two rounds. Reload and reengage each target with another two rounds. Start position is wrists above shoulders. Scoring is Virginia Count (no extra shots allowed, without penalty).

Focus:

This classifier is essentially a "distance change-up" type of drill that has easier targets mixed in with a very high risk target in the back.

Goal:

Try to shoot 10 percent above your current classification.

Commentary:

This classifier is an excellent test of your ability to "change gears." The back target requires you to fire four perfect shots on it. You don't need to be particularly fast on that target, but you do need to be fast everywhere else.

I think that a 5.5-second run on this stage is pretty quick. You don't need to worry too much about dropping points on this classifier. It isn't because the shots are easy; it is because you will either shoot "A"s, or you will get misses. It is as simple as that.

It seems most sensible to run the stage either right to left or left to right, and that will mean drawing on either of the closer partial targets. Those targets are easy, because you can aim off the center of the "A" zone a little bit. You will increase the odds of hitting a "C," but dramatically reduce your chances of clipping a no-shoot.

Of course, the make-or-break target is the back target. There is simply no way around it; you need to be accurate. There are a couple things I like to do to help my shooting. First, I make sure I fire each shot *individually*. There can't be any hint of a "double tap," or I might send one into the hard cover. It seems like it takes forever to let the sights settle for the second shot, but it isn't as long as it seems like (if you actually look at the timer). It is time well spent. The other thing that may help is to aim for the exact center of the "A" zone, not the whole thing. I like to pick an area about the size of a golf ball, and drive my sights to that.

One other important pitfall to recognize here is the danger the no-shoot targets pose. They don't make the actual shooting all that difficult during the stage, but they are positioned in a way that makes it very possible to drag your shots into the no-shoot if you move the gun too early off of one of them, or get on the trigger too early as you transition onto the other. Take care not to do that.

At the end of the day, this classifier is a good way to challenge yourself. There isn't anything difficult about it, but it strings together different elements in such a way that you need to be very competent in order to put up a good score.

Suggested Micro Drills:
Engage each target with two rounds.

Engage the close target with two rounds, reload, and reengage with two rounds.

Chapter 6
MOVEMENT SKILLS

The drills here are designed to help you move through your standard "run and gun" stage more efficiently. Before you can understand how to set these drills up, you need to understand a few of the key concepts behind them.

These drills are designed to isolate particular elements of your shooting, and help you learn to perform those elements better. No matter which drill you pick, you are working on a specific skill. After you look through the drills and read the commentary, it should be clear what it is you are supposed to be focused on.

Due to the relatively complex nature of these drills, they are all variable setup drills. You have complete control over target distances and so forth. That having been said, you need to pay careful attention to the setup notes to make sure you set the difficulty to something that is appropriate for you. If you set up the targets improperly, you could end up destroying the purpose of the drill. So, even though the drills are variable setup, you still need to set them up sensibly.

The drills are also designed to be adapted to your specific situation. You can run them left to right, right to left, front to back, and so on. You absolutely should not try to replicate the actual diagram. Use the diagram to get an idea of the skill you are working on, then set up an appropriate drill tailored to your actual range situation. For example, if your bay isn't deep enough to get a really long distance shot, use a partial target instead. Use your intelligence to set up the drills to do what they need to do.

You might be thinking that all of this sounds a little bit goofy. All of the drills in the marksmanship training and standard exercises sections are set up to be repeatable. The way these drills are, they will not be repeatable. I can't give you goal times, and you will not be tracking your progress over time. The reasoning behind this is that these drills are designed to help you learn to navigate field courses. In a match situation, you never see the same thing twice. I have experimented with repeatable setups for movement training, and frankly they just don't get the job done. It is, in my opinion, more effective to learn to apply skills on a constantly changing setup. If you keep working through new challenges, you will evolve more quickly as a shooter.

The other thing I should point out is that you should have plenty of data from the marksmanship training and standard exercises sections regarding the appropriate times. You should know how long a draw takes at whatever distance. You should know appropriate split times at whatever distance. You will have a good idea of what transition times should look like. So, you may not be able to know beforehand what an appropriate time for an entire drill will be, but you should have a good understanding of what your discrete skills should be. More simply put, you should know how long most things should take you. You will need to go through the timer and check to make sure you are running an appropriate time for yourself.

Another important thing I should point out is that most of the diagrams utilize shooting boxes. I used shooting boxes because I think most people will end up using them, but you don't have to. You can mark a spot on the ground using a cone, a stick, or anything you like. You don't need to follow the diagrams. As a matter of fact, I think it is best to use a vision barrier instead of a shooting box. Using a vision barrier to force yourself to move to a different position so you can see another target is a much more accurate representation of what you will actually see in matches. The only reason not to use them all the time is because they can be a pain in the ass to set up. If you have the time and equipment, use vision barriers.

Once again, I want to emphasize that these diagrams are broad outlines. You can use metric or classic targets. You can use poppers and plates. You can use whatever targets you want. The key is to set up the exercise so you are working on the skill that is outlined. Be creative, you will learn more. Essentially, the diagrams are just examples.

This may seem obvious, but once you shoot a drill, pay attention to your time. You can establish a "baseline time," and then work to improve that time. For example, if you start out running a drill in about six seconds, then through working at it you are going to attempt to improve that time. Fair warning, improving your time a little bit through practice that day doesn't mean much. You will almost always go a bit faster after you are "warmed up." Ideally, you get faster *and* learn how to refine your skills in the future.

Finally, once you get good at the drills in this section, I recommend you go to Chapter 8: Designing Practice Stages. In that section, you will essentially learn to string together two or more of these drills into a practice stage.

Position Entry

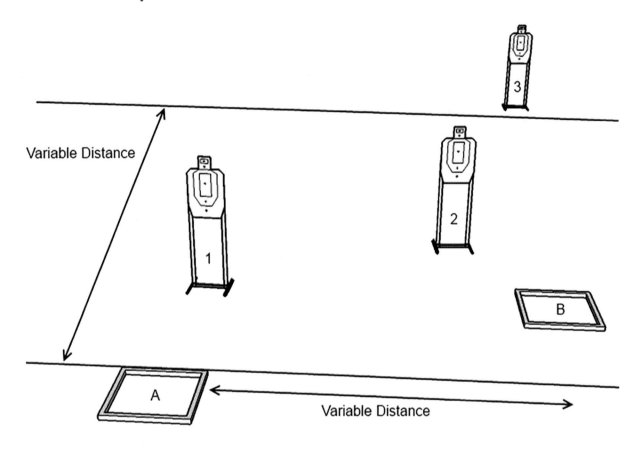

Variable Distance

Variable Distance

Date:	Par Time:	Notes:
	NA	
	NA	
	NA	
	NA	
	NA	
	NA	
	NA	
	NA	
	NA	
	NA	

Variable Setup:

This is a "variable setup" drill. I outline a concept for a drill, and then you can construct it based on your own situation. Do not attempt to recreate the diagram. You should create the scenario outlined in the setup notes. The "How to Use This Book" section has more information on variable setups.

Setup Notes:

This drill requires two shooting positions. From the first position you engage the specified targets and get moving. From the second shooting position, you will need an "easy" target to get set up on. What I mean by this is that you have a target that is sufficiently easy to make you feel comfortable shooting it while moving. By "set up" I mean you will (ideally) shoot that target as you are getting into the second position.

I like to put enough distance between Position A and Position B that there is an incentive to get running a little bit. Five yards or so is about right.

I prefer to use vision barriers instead of boxes for this drill.

Procedure:

Engage Target 1 from Box A. Engage Targets 2 and 3 from Box B. Use any desired start position.

Focus:

This drill is for developing your ability to get into a shooting position and being ready to shoot when you get there.

Goal:

You want to break your first shot on Target 2 as soon as you are "legal" to shoot (per USPSA rules) if using a shooting box. If you set up the drill using a vision barrier, you want to break your first shot on Target 2 as soon as you can see it.

Commentary:

This drill is the first one listed in the field course section for a reason. It is extremely important to master. Just to be clear, the important thing here is to be ready to shoot when you get to Position B. That means you have your gun up and ready to go, but it also means more than that. Not only should your gun be up and ready to go, but you should be aiming at the first target you are going to shoot from Position B. If you are using a vision barrier rather than a box, you can aim the gun at the wall in front of you at the spot where the target will appear. As soon as your sights clear the obstruction, you should be ready to fire.

On the timer, you should pay attention to the time between Target 1 and Target 2. That is the time you really want to make sure you work to improve. Running faster probably won't help, but breaking your first shot from Position B just a hair sooner will make a difference on the timer.

In terms of accuracy, you should strive for all "A"s. If you move into Position B extremely aggressively, you will likely see your shots start to hit a bit high or a bit low. This is due to the gun bouncing up and down as you move into position. If you bend your knees a bit more, it may improve your stability.

Finally, one thing that will not necessarily show up on the timer, but is in an important consideration, is the stance you end up in at Position B. It is a very bad habit to end up off balance or shooting the targets at an awkward angle. It may not cause issues on this day using this drill (depending on how difficult you make the targets in Position B), but you want to be sure you are building good habits. I recommend looking down at your feet and checking your stance at the end of every run to make sure your feet are where you want them.

Variations:

The most important variation here is whether or not to include a reload. If you are interested in making sure your reloads are solid,

go ahead and do one in between positions. I will caution you with this: If you aren't able to get your reload done in the space between Positions A and B, then you will absolutely defeat the purpose of this drill. If the reload isn't done, then you (by definition) can't be ready to shoot.

Another thing you may want to try is using one of the targets that is set almost all the way down to the ground. Those targets are usually set on a 45-degree angled stand. You see them often enough; they are worth trying.

Position Exit

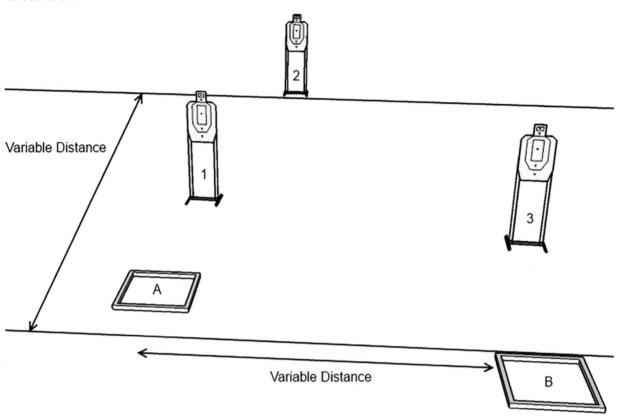

Date:	Par Time:	Notes:
	NA	
	NA	
	NA	
	NA	
	NA	
	NA	
	NA	
	NA	
	NA	
	NA	

Variable Setup:

This is a "variable setup" drill. I outline a concept for a drill and then you can construct it based on your own situation. Do not attempt to recreate the diagram. You should create the scenario outlined in the setup notes. The

"How to Use This Book" section has more information on variable setups.

Setup Notes:

This drill requires two shooting positions. As usual, vision barriers are preferable to boxes. What you need to set up is a drill where you engage at least two targets from Position A, and at least one target from Position B. The targets from Position A need to be "easy," so you, at your skill level, are able to comfortably shoot those targets while moving. The difficulty of the target in Position B isn't really an issue.

Procedure:

From Position A, engage the designated targets. Move to Position B and engage the designated target. The start position can be any desired position.

Focus:

This drill is designed to help you move out of a position while you are still shooting.

Goal:

The goal is to get moving from Position A as soon as possible. This means you are already moving your feet while you engage the last target.

Commentary:

This drill is a good one to learn the basics of getting out of a position.

I like to remind myself that good movement in USPSA doesn't come down to foot speed; it comes down to efficiency. The idea here is to get your movement started while you are still shooting. So, in essence, the movement part won't change; you are simply going to start it sooner.

As always, I like to make sure my knees are bent, and I use them as shock absorbers. I want to keep a nice stable sight picture so I am able to be accurate as I get out of that position.

I also like to break up the movement when I leave into two categories:

First, if you are shifting your weight toward Position B as you are firing, that counts as moving. Getting your center of gravity going certainly helps save time. Shifting your weight and getting your body moving will show up in your shoulders. Just get your shoulders headed toward Position B.

The second category is actually moving your feet. This is much tougher than simply shifting your weight, because as your feet come up off the ground, it will usually disturb your sight picture to a much larger extent.

In any event, you should do a good deal of experimentation with this drill to figure out what is going to work for you and what isn't. Everyone is a bit different and is set up (physically) in a little bit different way. You always want to be paying attention to your technique.

Variations:

One variation here is whether or not to include a reload. If you are interested in making sure your reloads are solid, then go ahead and do one in between positions.

Another thing to play around with is the target placement in Position A. You can place the targets so you need to "back out" of position to get headed toward Position B, or you can place them so you move in a forward direction, or a lateral direction. The way you construct this drill is important, because you need to make sure you construct it to work in all directions.

Short Moves

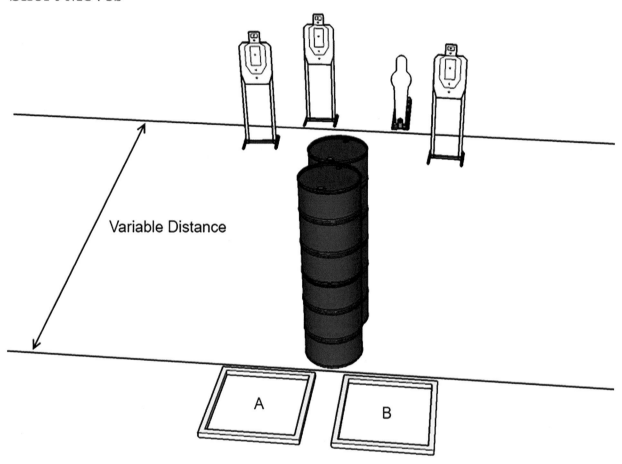

Date:	Par Time:	Notes:
	NA	
	NA	
	NA	
	NA	
	NA	
	NA	
	NA	
	NA	
	NA	
	NA	

Variable Setup:

This is a "variable setup" drill. I outline a concept for a drill and then you can construct it based on your own situation. Do not attempt to recreate the diagram. You should create the scenario outlined in the setup notes. The "How to Use This Book" section has more information on variable setups.

Setup Notes:

This drill requires a small shooting area requiring you to move two or three steps in order to hit all the targets. I prefer to use a wall section or something similar as a vision barrier in order to force a bit of movement.

Procedure:

Engage all targets as you move through the shooting area. The start position can be any desired position.

Focus:

The focus here is on making quick moves from one position to another without dismounting your gun.

Goal:

Move as aggressively as possible, and have the gun stabilized and ready to fire immediately.

Commentary:

This scenario covers short movements from one spot to another. I would set this up so your firing positions are two or three steps apart. Longer movements are covered in other scenarios. These shorter movements are

important because they are handled differently in terms of technique.

Most importantly, the gun should stay up high for the entirety of the drill. Keep the gun at your eyeline looking to the next target as you move. If possible, get a sight picture on the next target that you plan to engage before you are stable enough to engage it. I pay careful attention to that sight picture, and when it is stable enough to start firing, I get on with it. Being able to shoot sooner is, in many ways, dependent on how difficult you make the target scenario.

The other focal point here is getting a good "push" from one spot to another. Keep both of your feet planted firmly on the ground until it is time to move. When you move, push with both feet aggressively to the other side of your shooting area. As you get set up in your second firing position, use your legs to get stabilized quickly. You shouldn't have a feeling of being off balance or falling over.

Variations:

If you wish, you can do a variation of this where you reload between firing positions. If you choose to reload, then it will likely restrict how aggressively you can move from one spot to the other. Pushing 100 percent as hard as you can will mean you get to where you need to go with the reload still not finished. That will not really serve you. Instead, I recommend that you back off your movement aggression level just a little, and focusing on getting your reload finished.

Shooting on the Move

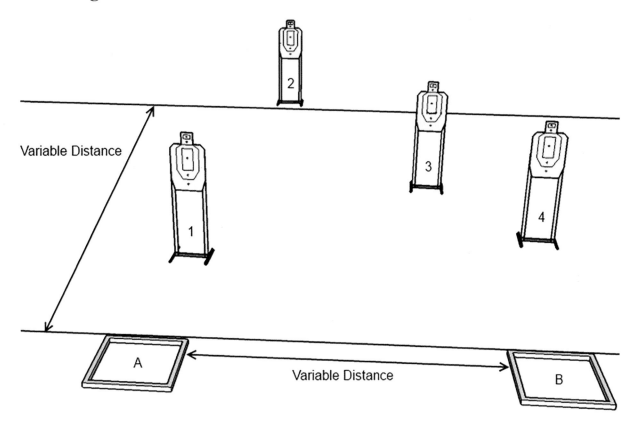

Date:	Par Time:	Notes:
	NA	
	NA	
	NA	
	NA	
	NA	
	NA	
	NA	
	NA	
	NA	
	NA	

Variable Setup:

This is a "variable setup" drill. I outline a concept for a drill, and then you can construct it based on your own situation. Do not attempt to recreate the diagram. You should create the scenario outlined in the setup notes. The

"How to Use This Book" section has more information on variable setups.

Setup Notes:

This drill requires two shooting positions. As usual, vision barriers are preferable to boxes. What you need to set up is a drill where all the targets, except the final one (Target 4 in the above example), are available from anywhere. One target is available only from Position B. The difficulty of the target in Position B isn't really an issue. The rest of the targets should all be targets that you, at your skill level, find easy to shoot "A"s on, even while moving. Put a substantial amount of distance between Position A and Position B, at least 10 yards.

Procedure:

Start in Position A. At the signal, draw and engage Targets 1-3 from any desired location. Engage Target 4 from Position B and only Position B.

Focus:

Refine your shooting while moving.

Goal:

The goal is to be able to move at just about a flat run and still hit "A"s on the targets.

Commentary:

This drill should help you shoot while moving. If the procedure is in some way unclear, the intent is that you start at Position A, then move to Position B in order to engage the one target stipulated to be engaged from there.

The other targets are available on the way to Position B, and it is my intent that you engage them on the way. Of course, you could just run to Position B and engage all the targets from there, but that would undermine the purpose of the drill (it does make for an interesting experiment if you are calculating hit factors though).

The reason that there is a lot of distance between Position A and Position B is that you need to move hard and fast in order to put up a good time on this drill. That makes the shooting part kind of tricky.

It may be tempting to do a very conservative "roll step" on this drill, but honestly, it is just too slow. The best hit factors are going to be produced by putting the gas pedal down and *moving*. If you are too conservative, you just waste too much time.

On the other hand, you probably know that no matter how fast you run, you aren't going to outrun a bunch of points down. A couple "C"s may well be acceptable on a stage like this, but "D"s and misses are not.

If this is sounding like you need to learn to run a tightrope between being in control and shooting like your hair is on fire, then you are right. I suggest calculating hit factors until you get the hang of things. Cutting a couple seconds off by shooting with a target focus (or a similar strategy) may well drop you more points, but usually it is worth it if you calculate the hit factor.

Finally, there is another thing I like to consider on a drill like this, and that is the amount of "dead time" that I have. If you find yourself finished with shooting the targets, and then running a few paces to Position B, you may want to consider spending a bit more time aiming at the targets you are shooting while moving. This can be largely setup dependent. If you have things set so that you have lots of distance to cover between Position A and Position B, then there may well be no way you can use all of that time productively.

Variations:

The biggest variable here is the distance between Position A and Position B. I strongly recommend you play around with the distance and note the effect it has on your points and time. You will see everything in matches from taking a couple steps and having three targets to engage in that time, or making a 30-yard run with a few targets sprinkled in. You want to be ready for anything, so it certainly pays to be prepared.

Of course, you can always work in a reload at some point in the drill if you want to practice that.

Finally, I think it is useful to work in a distance changeup. Having a couple very easy targets followed by a target you really need to aim at is a reflection of a challenge you can certainly expect to encounter in a match situation. Stapling a no-shoot up on one of the targets in this drill after you get bored with the way you have it set up will reinvigorate your practice session.

Moving Reload

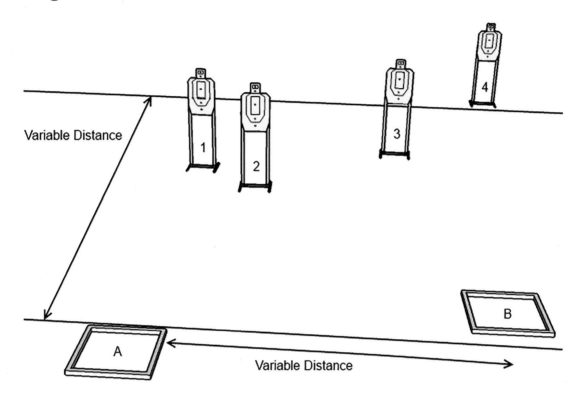

Date:	Par Time:	Notes:
	NA	
	NA	
	NA	
	NA	
	NA	
	NA	
	NA	
	NA	
	NA	
	NA	

Variable Setup:

This is a "variable setup" drill. I outline a concept for a drill, and then you can construct it based on your own situation. Do not attempt to recreate the diagram. You should create the scenario outlined in the setup notes. The "How to Use This Book" section has more information on variable setups.

Setup Notes:

This drill requires two shooting positions. As usual, vision barriers are preferable to boxes. What you need to set up is a drill where all the targets except the final one (Target 4 in the above example) are available from anywhere. One target is available only from Position B. The difficulty of the target in Position B isn't really an issue. The rest of the targets should all be targets that you, at your skill level, find easy to shoot "A"s on, even while moving. Put a substantial amount of distance between Position A and Position B, at least 10 yards.

Procedure:

Start at Position A. Use any desired start position. At the signal, engage Target 1 and Target 2. Execute a reload, then engage Target 3. Finally, engage Target 4 from Position B. You are allowed to engage Targets 1-3 from any location.

Focus:

Execute efficient reloads while moving, and continue to engage targets.

Goal:

I like to have my reload time on this drill run within 0.1 to 0.2 seconds of a static reload on an equally distant target.

Commentary:

This drill is similar to the "Shooting on the Move" drill from earlier in this section, but it works in a reload.

What you are working on here is your "flow." It is frequently the case that shooters stop moving when they reload or look really "herky-jerky" while shooting. All this drill requires is that you move from Position A to Position B while shooting and reloading; that's it. You don't need to be especially fast to put up a good time, you just need to be efficient.

The specific focus of this drill is your reload. The idea here is to have as little "downtime" as possible. The instant you finish the first two targets, your focus should shift to the reload. As soon as that is done, you are back up on target and shooting.

The reason I think this drill is important is that most shooters conceptualize reloading as something that happens when you run from one spot to the next. Since there is a target that needs to be engaged straight away after reloading, you don't need to worry about running. In my experience, this scenario is more common than running 10 yards while you stuff a new mag in the gun. Most field courses have the next target available after just a few steps, so this drill should prepare you to get the gun loaded and ready to go right away.

Pay careful attention to the distance of Target 3 from the firing line. Make a mental note of that distance, and think about what reload times you would run on a static drill in the standard exercises section. You should be very close to your static reload time. For example, if you can usually run a 1.1 or 1.2-second reload at the seven yard line, then you should run a 1.2 or 1.3 reload on a seven-yard target in this drill.

Variations:

I think it is important for you to run this drill both left to right and right to left. You don't want to risk a disqualification in a match situation, so be prepared to reload while moving in any direction.

Hitting the Spot

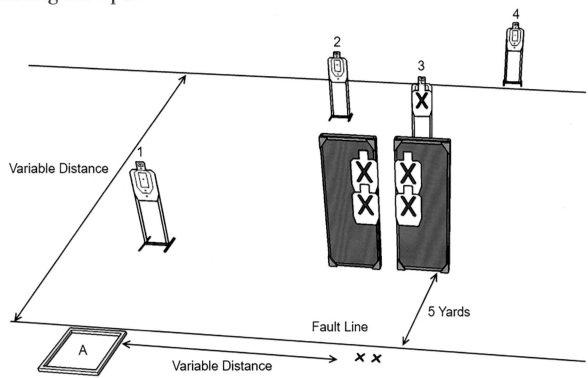

Date:	Par Time:	Notes:
	NA	
	NA	
	NA	
	NA	
	NA	
	NA	
	NA	
	NA	
	NA	
	NA	

Variable Setup:

This is a "variable setup" drill. I outline a concept for a drill, and then you can construct it based on your own situation. Do not attempt to recreate the diagram. You should create the scenario outlined in the setup notes. The "How to Use This Book" section has more information on variable setups.

Setup Notes:

This scenario requires a starting position (Box A). It also requires a narrow set of vision barriers. You can use two barricades, and then place them so there is a six-inch slit between them. You will also need to place a fault line five yards uprange of the slit.

Place one target in front of Box A and place the other targets so they are visible through the slit while standing uprange of the fault line.

Procedure:

Start in Box A. Use any desired start position. Engage Target 1 from any desired location. Engage all other targets through the slit while remaining uprange of the fault line.

Focus:

Pay careful attention to your positioning. You want to efficiently hit the spot, or position, required to be able to see the targets through the slit.

Goal:

Move into the required position to engage the targets through the slit with no hesitation and minimal shuffling around.

Commentary:

This exercise is designed to prepare you to get set up in a very specific location. Generally speaking, you don't need to be very careful in matches about the exact location of the shooting positions. They may have a port or a large free-fire zone. It is easy to find each location. This drill prepares you for the somewhat less common but more difficult scenario in which you need to locate very specific spots and shoot from them efficiently.

This drill is named "Hitting the Spot" for good reason. If you set it up correctly, you are going to need to be in *exactly* the right location in order to get your hits on a target. If you move a few inches in either direction, you won't be able to see the target through the slit, and you are going to waste time shuffling around looking for the target.

When shooting this drill, you should strive for a smooth engagement sequence with no hunting for your foot position or target location. You may be surprised at just how much time you can burn up by being even slightly out of position. You will find that being extremely aggressive with your movements may make it harder to hit your positions with precision. This is a game of finesse, not brute force.

I like to find markers on the ground to indicate where I need to place my feet in order to find the targets. This necessitates doing a walkthrough just like you would in an actual match. Take the time to scope out the scenario and plan out your positioning. You will need to bring the planning element to matches, not just the technical skills to shoot the targets.

As with any drill requiring movement, it is critical to have your gun up in position ready to shoot as soon as possible. I find it helpful to aim through the wall at the target I plan on engaging, and as soon as my sights clear the wall, I should be able to start shooting. It isn't about moving fast, it is about shooting sooner.

Depending on how you set up the targets through the slit, you may need to reposition in order to engage them all. You should strive to reposition as few times as possible. Each time you set up, you are going to be burning up time.

Variations:

I recommend changing the slit width. You can make it as tight as just a couple inches, or perhaps make it much more generous. Note the effect that changing the slit has on your times. As you make the positioning more and more difficult, note the effect this has. Tightening the slit up enough may make it a serious marksmanship challenge (that is why I added no-shoot targets to the slit in the diagram).

Another element that is important is the fault line location. Moving the fault line further from the slit will make things tougher, and moving it closer makes things easier. I encourage you to make things challenging. You want to practice on scenarios that are less demanding than what you will actually face in a match situation.

Also, spreading the targets in the slit out more will make for a much more complicated scenario. Splitting them up far enough may require you to take a different position for each and every one of them.

Finally, you can put the start box further away from the fault line in order to give yourself a little bit of a run. You may find as you start running further that it is more difficult to put on the brakes and finesse your way into the correct position. Overrunning your position is a real possibility if you get a big enough head of steam built up.

Lean

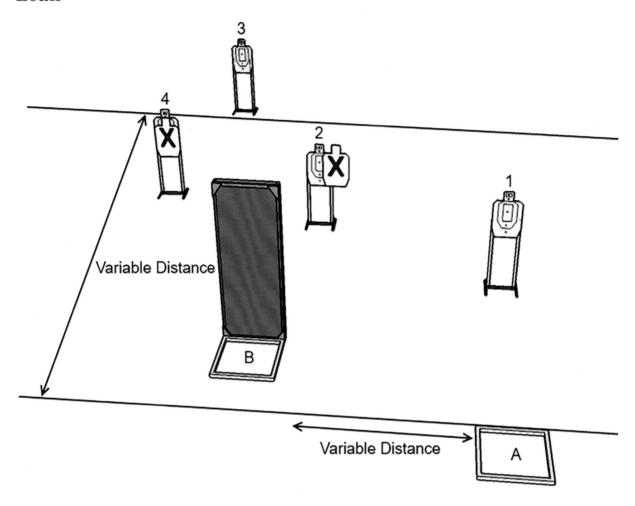

Date:	Par Time:	Notes:
	NA	
	NA	
	NA	
	NA	
	NA	
	NA	
	NA	
	NA	
	NA	
	NA	

Variable Setup:

This is a "variable setup" drill. I outline a concept for a drill, and then you can construct it based on your own situation. Do not attempt to recreate the diagram. You should create the scenario outlined in the setup notes. The "How to Use This Book" section has more information on variable setups.

Setup Notes:

This drill requires two shooting positions. What you need to set up is a drill where you engage at least one target from Position A, and at least two targets from Position B. Position B needs to be constructed in such a way that there is a barricade forcing you to lean somewhat in order to engage the required targets. It is entirely up to your discretion to determine how much to force yourself to lean.

Procedure:

Start at Position A in any desired start position.

Engage Target 1 from Position A. Move to Position B and engage Targets 2-4.

Focus:

This drill is focused on learning how to effectively position your body for positions requiring a lean.

Goal:

The goal for this drill is to get into Position B quickly, be ready to shoot when you get there, and engage those targets with a minimum of repositioning.

Commentary:

This drill is a good way to learn to manage positions that require a lean. You see positions like that in virtually every match, so obviously it is something that you want to work on.

The whole idea here is to minimize the effect of the actual barricade. If possible (depending on the way you construct the drill), you want to stay back from the barricade. You want to have your upper body in as comfortable a position as possible. It is as important as ever to perform a walkthrough on this drill, just to figure out the ideal positioning. Every match situation is a little bit different, and part of this drill is getting used to coming up with a plan.

When you are sorting out the right position, you also want to pay close attention to your feet. I find that usually when I get the outside foot exactly where it needs to be and pointed in the right direction, then the rest of my body lines up how I want it. By "outside" foot, I am referring to the foot you need to lean on to.

Depending on how far you need to lean, this can really turn into a patience drill. The more you disrupt your regular shooting position, the more you need to make sure that the sights are returning to the target. If you set up tight partial targets, the difficulty of this drill will magnify quickly.

Variations:

It is essential to change this drill up.

First, I like to alternate what side of the barricade I am allowed to shoot from. You can require shooting from the left, the right, or allow yourself to go whichever way you prefer based on the situation. If you go based on the situation, then you go whichever way you think is fastest/easiest based on the way you have the targets laid out.

Next, move the targets around. Work on everything from a minimal lean to an extremely difficult lean that you are barely capable of. Don't worry about making things too hard. If you prepare yourself for anything you could see in matches, you will be in good shape.

Finally, work on many different target difficulties. A bit of a lean on a very difficult target can make things very tough. A tight enough lean can double the difficulty of any given target. On the other hand, a lean may not change a thing on the close targets. Be ready for everything.

Port Setup

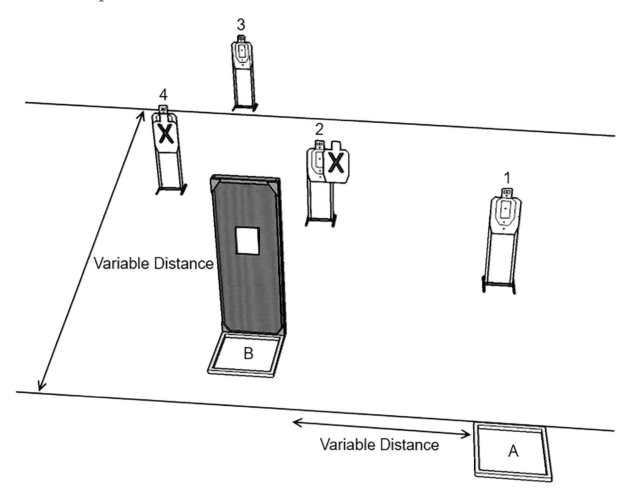

Date:	Par Time:	Notes:
	NA	
	NA	
	NA	
	NA	
	NA	
	NA	
	NA	
	NA	
	NA	
	NA	

Variable Setup:

This is a "variable setup" drill. I outline a concept for a drill, and then you can construct it based on your own situation. Do not attempt to recreate the diagram. You should create the scenario outlined in the setup notes. The "How to Use This Book" section has more information on variable setups.

Setup Notes:

This drill requires two shooting positions. Position A is just a spot on the ground or a box. That will be the start position. Position B is a shooting port. I usually use a target with the "A" zone cut out of it to create the shooting port, but you can improvise whatever you want based on your specific situation.

What you need to set up is a scenario where all the targets, except the first one (Target 1 in the above example), are available from the port. Put a substantial amount of distance between Position A and Position B, around five yards should be fine.

The difficulty for Targets 2-4 is up to your discretion. I recommend setting a mix of difficulties and doing some experimentation.

Procedure:

Start at Position A. Use any desired start position. At the signal, engage Target 1. Move to Position B and engage all remaining targets.

Focus:

The idea here is to learn to deal with ports. You should be able to engage targets through a port while allowing the vision barrier caused by the port to minimally disrupt your shooting.

Goal:

Depending on the construction of the scenario, you should try to get the same time/points as you would if you were shooting from a box rather than shooting through a port. This is not a reasonable goal if you construct the port in such a way as to make the shooting more difficult.

Commentary:

Ports are a fact of life at USPSA matches. Many match directors use ports the same way that they used to use shooting boxes. They force you to engage targets from a specific position by making them only available through a shooting port. In some other situations, the ports are actually used to add difficulty to the shooting scenario. By making the port low to the ground, very narrow, or by forcing you into an awkward position, it can stack difficulty onto the shots in a big hurry.

When the shooting isn't more difficult, you want to be able to shoot at the same pace that you otherwise would if you were just standing out in the open. There are a few tricks to this.

First, you need to carefully plan out your positioning. If the scenario you have set up requires your feet to be in a very specific spot, then take the time to figure out where that spot is, and find a marker on the ground, eye level, or anyplace to help you locate that spot when you are in a hurry.

Next, be ready to shoot when you get to the port. Have the gun up and be aiming at the first target you plan to shoot. You should get a sight picture on the target even if the wall is in the way of you actually seeing the target. As soon as your sights clear the vision barrier, you should be clear to shoot. If the target is more difficult, then you will need to let your sights settle down just a little bit more.

Finally, you may need to shift your feet around a little bit in order to get all the targets through the port. This will happen if you set the targets up spaced far enough apart. If this happens, then preplan the move from one position to the next.

If there is one more piece of advice to give, it is that you will transition best from one target to the next if you can see the target you plan to transition to from your position. This means that it is best to plan things so you can always at least see the edge of the next target. If you can't see it, you will usually end up hunting around for it. Pay attention to your target transition times in the port, and work to reduce them.

Variations:

There are a few things you should absolutely change during the course of this drill.

Play around with the height of the port. Comfortable standing height should not be the only way you practice. Change it up!

Change the dimensions of the port by making it very small, large, or odd shapes. Anything you can think of may be helpful. I have seen ports as small as a two-inch circle in matches, so don't make it easy on yourself.

Play with the position of fault lines behind you. Again, don't make it easy. Comfortably standing in a free-fire zone is a whole different thing than being confined to a narrow shooting area set at a strange angle.

Low Port

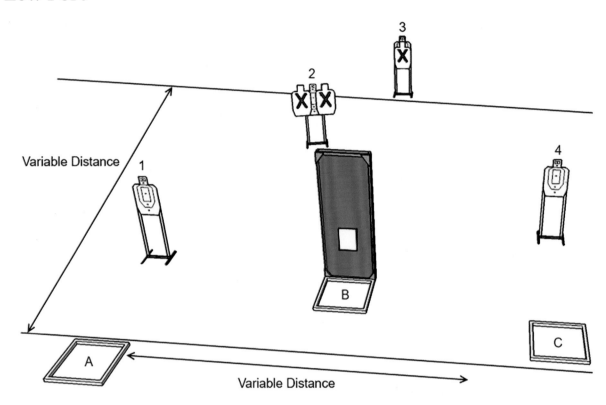

Date:	Par Time:	Notes:
	NA	
	NA	
	NA	
	NA	
	NA	
	NA	
	NA	
	NA	
	NA	
	NA	

Variable Setup:

This is a "variable setup" drill. I outline a concept for a drill, and then you can construct it based on your own situation. Do not attempt to recreate the diagram. You should create the scenario outlined in the setup notes. The "How to Use This Book" section has more information on variable setups.

Setup Notes:

This drill requires three shooting positions. Positions A and C are just spots on the ground or boxes. These are the starting and ending positions. Position B is a low shooting port. I usually use a target with the "A" zone cut out of it to create the shooting port, but you can improvise whatever you want based on your specific situation. The port needs to be set low enough toward the ground to disrupt your shooting stance. I prefer to have them low enough that I feel uncomfortable shooting through them.

What you need to set up is a scenario where Targets 2 and 3 are available from the port. Put a substantial amount of distance between the shooting positions, at least five yards.

The difficulty for Targets 2 and 3 is up to your discretion. I recommend setting a mix of difficulties, and doing some experimentation.

One safety note here: Be sure that the targets are positioned in such a way that when you engage them from the low port, you aren't sending rounds over the berm. You need to have a safe backstop for all rounds fired.

Procedure:

Start at Position A. Engage Target 1 from Position A. Move to Position B and engage Targets 2 and 3. Move to Position C and engage Target 4.

Use any desired start position. You may start in Position C and run the stage in reverse order.

Focus:

The focus here is to flow in and out of the low port smoothly.

Goal:

Move into the port efficiently, set up efficiently, and get out of the port quickly.

Commentary:

I pay particular attention to a few different things when working this drill.

First, you should monitor the times between positions. Look to be breaking your first shot in the low port as soon as you can and look to get out of that position smoothly and efficiently.

Pay close attention to your positioning in the port. You want to be able to make the shots with a minimum of shifting around or delay. I like to have my gun up, ready to go, in the low port long before I am ready to shoot. That way I am working on sight alignment as early as I can.

Since you need to get out of the low port, you may notice a big time difference between squatting and kneeling in that position. Putting a knee down is usually comfortable and stable, but it does add some time. As you vary the port height, you will see what sort of position you can get away with.

Of course, it should go without saying that you need to keep the gun in a safe position while you work on this drill. Get in the habit of having the gun not only safe, but very clearly safe. You don't want the range officer to have any questions about your safety when you are at a match, so pay attention to that during your training.

Variations:

There are a few important elements here that you should make sure to play around with.

First, you should vary the port. You can change the height, width, the distance from the ground, and you can even put fault lines down to keep yourself well away from the port or force you to cram your body right up against the wall.

You can vary the target arrangements. You can spread the targets out really wide so there is quite a bit of transitioning. You can use wide open targets, partials, steel, or a mix of all of the above.

You can change the distance from position to position. A longer run will be a little bit different than a quick little two-step move.

Port to Port

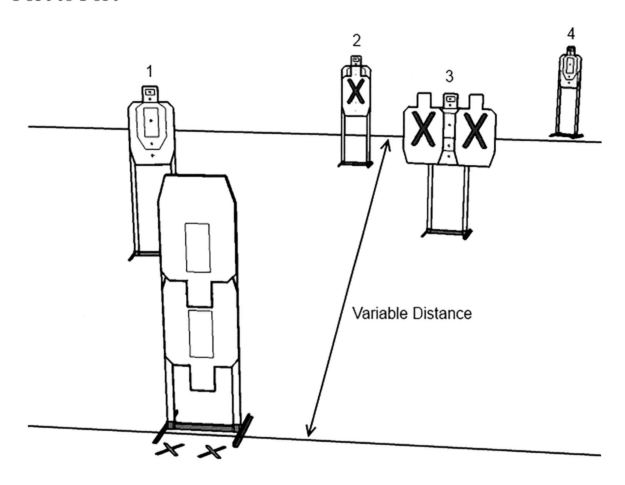

Variable Distance

Date:	Par Time:	Notes:
	NA	
	NA	
	NA	
	NA	
	NA	
	NA	
	NA	
	NA	
	NA	
	NA	

Variable Setup:

This is a "variable setup" drill. I outline a concept for a drill, and then you can construct it based on your own situation. Do not attempt to recreate the diagram. You should create the scenario outlined in the setup notes. The "How to Use This Book" section has more information on variable setups.

Setup Notes:

For this drill you will need to construct multiple (two) shooting ports. The easiest thing to do is to remove the "A" zone from a couple of targets and staple them to stands close together, or maybe even on the same stand. You can use those "A" zones as your shooting ports. I leave the difficulty of the targets to your discretion.

Procedure:

Start with your hands relaxed at sides, standing in the shooting area. Engage any two targets from one port, then engage the remaining targets from the other port.

Focus:

Pay careful attention to the time between the ports. You want to aggressively drive the gun from one to the next.

Goal:

The goal here is to navigate the ports with an absolute minimum of little bobbles or problems that add time. You want to spend zero time hunting around for the next target; smoothly transition from one target to the next and one port to the next.

Commentary:

It is sometimes the case that you will encounter a match director that seems absolutely obsessed with ports. This isn't exactly my favorite thing, but it is certainly a legitimate sort of challenge.

As with any vision barrier challenge, I really emphasize flowing through the target engagement sequence with a minimum of little bobbles or disruptions. The key thing here isn't to only set yourself up to shoot one port, but to set up for both ports simultaneously (if possible). In an ideal situation, you set your feet properly, and then simply transition through the targets.

Another important consideration here is to try and keep your gun out of the ports. If you need to pull the gun out of a port to transition to the next one, you are probably losing a little bit of time. Depending on how you construct this, it may not be possible to keep the gun out, but if it is, try and stay clear of the port. It is a natural tendency for people to want to hug up on walls and get deep into ports, but it isn't usually productive.

Variations:

The most important variation for a shooter, in a restricted capacity division, is to work on reloading between ports. It is a frequent occurrence in matches that you need to execute a reload where you essentially don't have any movement, but you just have to transition the gun from one port to the next while you reload. To simulate that scenario, you can work in a reload from port to port.

Prone

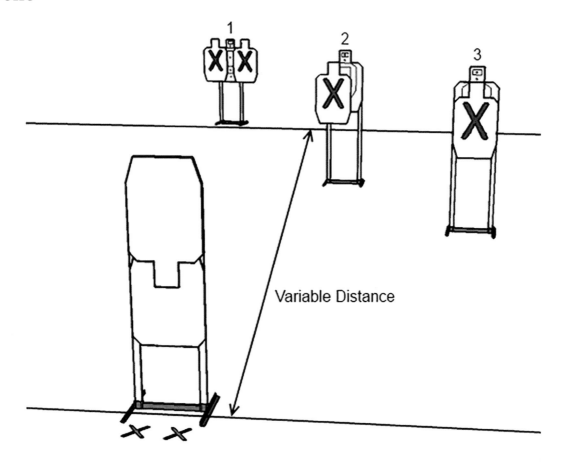

Date:	Par Time:	Notes:
	NA	
	NA	
	NA	
	NA	
	NA	
	NA	
	NA	
	NA	
	NA	
	NA	

Variable Setup:

This is a "variable setup" drill. I outline a concept for a drill, and then you can construct it based on your own situation. Do not attempt to recreate the diagram. You should create the scenario outlined in the setup notes. The "How to Use This Book" section has more information on variable setups.

Setup Notes:

Simply set up some targets of varying difficulties. Depending on the range surface, you may want to put down a blanket or some other padding on the ground to soften things up for yourself. Make the targets varying difficulties and various partial configurations as shown in the diagram.

Safety note: Make sure that your rounds impact the berm. It may not be possible to set the targets up high on the stands, depending on your range situation.

Procedure:

Start standing with your hands relaxed at sides. At the signal, go prone and engage each target with two rounds.

Focus:

Focus on developing your prone shooting skills, and being comfortable making any shot that may be required from that position.

Goal:

Your prone shooting practice should make you comfortable and proficient with getting into the prone position and making shots. You don't want to be afraid of this in a match situation.

Commentary:

Prone shooting is one of those things that most people don't like to practice, and most match directors don't like to use. However, if you want to take your game to the absolute top level, you need to be ready for anything. That dictates that you be ready to shoot prone.

Fundamentally, there is nothing different about shooting from the prone position. You line up the sights and pull the trigger just like everything else. On the other hand, there are quite a few little issues that you need to pay attention to when you are prone.

First, your arm position is really important. You need to figure out how to position your arms so you are stable enough for the shot required, but you also don't want to be burning up tons of time. I normally have my arms flat on the ground, with my head really low, so I can get on the sights. If the targets are closer and easier, I will select a less stable position (perhaps no contact with the ground using my arms).

You should also play around with your foot position. It isn't always an option in a match situation to put your feet wherever you want. There may be fault lines in the way. Get control of where you are putting your feet so you don't fault any lines.

You should figure out how to get down into the prone position in the first place. I look down to where I am putting my gun and line the rest of my body up off of that. There are other techniques and other ways of doing things. Don't let the match be the first time you try this.

Finally, you should figure out where your point of impact is when you are prone vs. standing. Most people experience a dramatic shift, causing them to hit low from the prone position. This is the reason for all the partial targets in this exercise. You need to know precisely where your bullets will impact.

Variations:

Obviously, you should vary everything from target distance and difficulty to how wide the transitions are between targets. Also, if you work a prone scenario into a practice stage, you should work at getting up from the position, and not just getting down.

Chapter 7
OTHER SKILLS

The drills here are designed to help you work through the miscellaneous challenges that you see at USPSA matches. Extremely difficult positions, single-handed shooting, and moving targets are some of the skills covered here.

This section isn't so much about pushing for really fast times, but it is about learning how to deal with any conceivable shooting situation that you may encounter in a competitive environment.

Empty Start

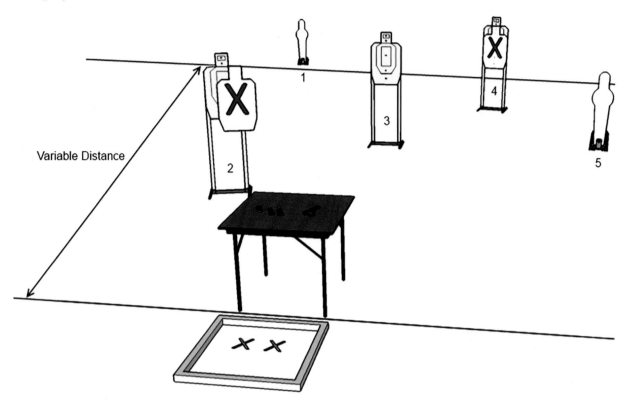

Date:	Par Time:	Notes:
	NA	
	NA	
	NA	
	NA	
	NA	
	NA	
	NA	
	NA	
	NA	
	NA	

Variable Setup:

This is a "variable setup" drill. I outline a concept for a drill, and then you can construct it based on your own situation. Do not attempt to recreate the diagram. You should create the scenario outlined in the setup notes. The "How to Use This Book" section has more information on variable setups.

Setup Notes:

This drill requires a table, barrel, or something else you can set your empty gun and filled magazines on. Other than that, you just need some variety of targets to shoot at. I like to mix in partial targets and steel, but I leave the details up to you.

Procedure:

Starting with your hands relaxed at sides, pick your gun up and load it, then engage all the targets. Start with your magazines laying near the gun.

Focus:

The most important thing here is a smooth and consistent load.

Goal:

Aggressively and smoothly load your gun. Finish that process with a good grip allowing you to quickly and effectively engage the targets.

Commentary:

At most major matches, they have at least one stage where you need to pick your gun up and load it. Sometimes, you can take a few steps while this is being done. Sometimes, you have targets to engage straight away. It depends on the circumstance.

You want to feel comfortable picking the gun up and getting it loaded. You should never have any anxiety about any of these scenarios. That is why you need to do a bit of practice.

As far as I am concerned, the key to success is going to be how good of a grip I get on the pistol when I pick it up, and how good of a grip I get on the magazine. If my grip is screwed up, things go downhill in a really big hurry.

At most matches, you aren't going to have control over where your gun gets placed. Usually, they will stipulate a position for the trigger guard. Sometimes, they make you put the magazine (or magazines) in specific locations as well. I recommend practicing with your gun placed where it feels awkward or uncomfortable to get to, just so you feel prepared for any scenario.

Finally, I am a lot more successful when I keep my hands and arms relaxed and ready to move. If I tense up (like under pressure in a match situation), I'll find my success rate goes down quite a bit. I like to "shake out" my arms and hands just before I get the start signal, so I feel loose and ready to move quickly.

Variations:

I think you should vary the position of the gun and the magazines as much as you possibly can. Don't forget to do a few runs with your magazine coming out of your pouches instead of off the table.

Table Start/Mag Stuff

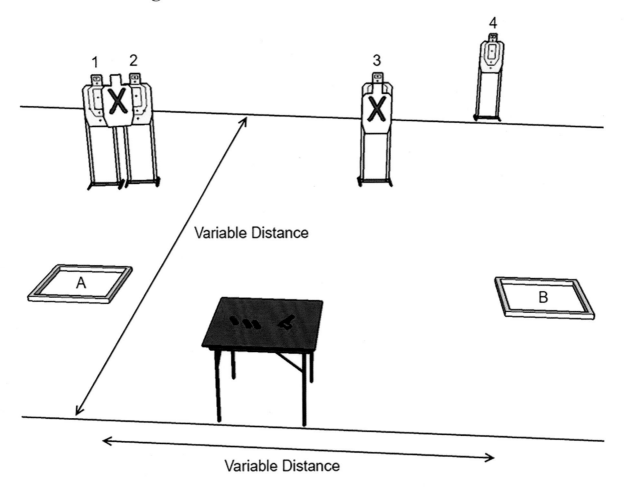

Date:	Par Time:	Notes:
	NA	
	NA	
	NA	
	NA	
	NA	
	NA	
	NA	
	NA	
	NA	
	NA	

Variable Setup:

This is a "variable setup" drill. I outline a concept for a drill, and then you can construct it based on your own situation. Do not attempt to recreate the diagram. You should create the scenario outlined in the setup notes. The "How to Use This Book" section has more information on variable setups.

Setup Notes:

This drill requires a table or a barrel. Anything you can stage your gun and magazines on will work fine. The only other thing required is a couple of shooting boxes or other markers. You could use vision barriers instead of shooting boxes to create your shooting positions.

Procedure:

Start standing with your hands relaxed at sides uprange of the table. Have your gun on the table unloaded and have all your magazines on the table. At the signal, pick up your gun and mags. Engage Targets 1 and 2 from Position A. Engage Targets 3 and 4 from Position B. Do a mandatory reload as you move from Position A to Position B.

Focus:

The focus here is getting used to grabbing your magazines and stuffing them in your pouches as you move to a shooting position.

Goal:

You want to have a "bobble-free" start to this practice stage, where you smoothly get your gun loaded and get ammunition stowed away. After that, you want to smoothly execute the shooting part of the stage.

Commentary:

This drill isn't an absolutely essential thing for you to practice, but it is a nice diversion from your regular training. If you want the extra little bit of confidence that comes along with having trained a little bit on every possible scenario, then this is a great thing to do.

When running this scenario, pay careful attention to how you actually stow the magazines away. If your division allows a magnet, then that will make things easy. If not, I recommend looking down at the pouch and actually looking the magazines into place. That seems to work the best based on the testing I have done.

You may experiment with how to do things. Do you load the gun, then stuff the ammo, or the other way around? Should you wait until you get mags in your pouches to rack the slide? Pretty much every time I go to a match with a stage like this, I see people confused by how to go about it. If you set up the same type of scenario in practice, then the confusion will be eliminated.

Variations:

If you like, you can force yourself to stuff more magazines into your pouches in the start position. This will help you simulate a stage where you perhaps have to pick up four magazines. You do occasionally see these things at major matches, and you want to be well prepared for it.

You may also want to try going back to the table for a magazine in between Positions A and B. It depends on how exactly you set the stage up, but sometimes it is a bit faster to do things that way. It is a good idea to experiment and get comfortable with all the options.

One-Handed Shooting

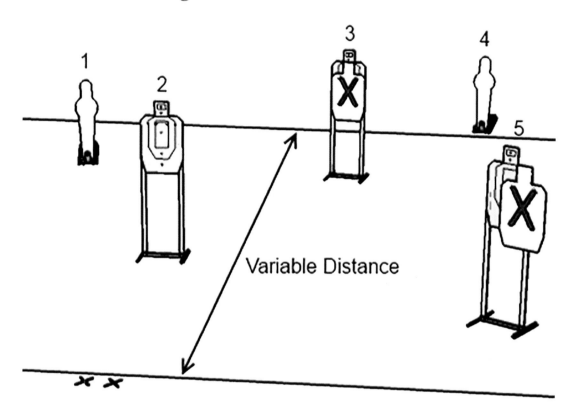

Date:	Par Time:	Notes:
	NA	
	NA	
	NA	
	NA	
	NA	
	NA	
	NA	
	NA	
	NA	
	NA	

Variable Setup:

This is a "variable setup" drill. I outline a concept for a drill, and then you can construct it based on your own situation. Do not attempt to recreate the diagram. You should create the scenario outlined in the setup notes. The "How to Use This Book" section has more information on variable setups.

Setup Notes:

This drill requires an assortment of different difficulty targets. Don't be shy about ramping up the difficulty level.

Procedure:

Start with your hands relaxed at sides. Draw and engage all the targets strong hand only **or** weak hand only.

Focus:

Develop your one-handed shooting skills.

Goal:

Be completely confident and comfortable that you can make any shot on demand with only one hand.

Commentary:

Single-handed shooting is a skill that most people don't practice a whole lot. If you want to consistently do well at major matches, you at least need to be proficient at this; there is no other way around it. You don't want your lack of skill in one area like this to take you out of the running at a match. You must be able to make any shot on demand. I see too many shooters picking up penalties during one-handed shooting, even when the shots aren't really that difficult.

If you are using a double-action gun, you have an additional wrinkle thrown into the mix. It can be difficult to be accurate when firing that first shot with a long and heavy pull. You may want to try starting on closer targets in order to minimize the difficulty. Again, you eventually need to make any shot with that double action trigger mode, but early on it can be helpful to start on easy stuff.

For me, the biggest thing I work on is making sure I nail the grip. When I draw to strong hand shooting or transfer the gun to my weak hand, I need to be careful to get a proper grip. If you nail that step down, it makes things so much easier.

Variations:

Be sure to try shooting while holding an object (such as a bag) in your non-firing hand. It is frequently the case in a match situation that the stage designer will force you to shoot with one hand by making you hold something, such as a rope or briefcase in the other hand. It is good to get used to that sensation during your training.

One-Handed Lean

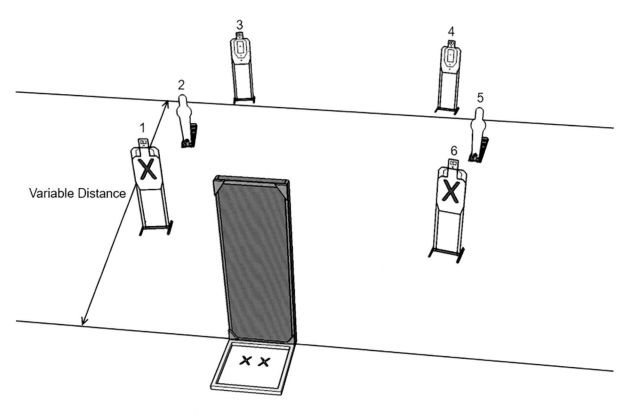

Date:	Par Time:	Notes:
	NA	
	NA	
	NA	
	NA	
	NA	
	NA	
	NA	
	NA	
	NA	
	NA	

Variable Setup:

This is a "variable setup" drill. I outline a concept for a drill, and then you can construct it based on your own situation. Do not attempt to recreate the diagram. You should create the scenario outlined in the setup notes. The "How to Use This Book" section has more information on variable setups.

Setup Notes:

This drill requires an assortment of targets with different difficulty. Don't be shy about ramping up the difficulty level.

Procedure:

Start with your hands relaxed at sides. Draw and engage all the targets strong hand only *or* weak hand only.

Focus:

Develop your one-handed shooting skills.

Goal:

Be completely confident and comfortable that you can make any shot on demand with only one hand.

Commentary:

Sometimes, you will need to shoot one-handed around a wall. The awkward position may be an issue for you, so become proficient during your training.

If you set the targets so that you have a hard time seeing them with both eyes when you are shooting, it will create an additional challenge. Depending on which eye is dominant, and all the other vision situations that people have, having the barricade obstructing one eye's view can be a real problem. The best time to experience this issue is in practice, so at least you can get a sense of it. I think the easiest thing to do is usually to lean out just a bit further so the barricade isn't in the way, but that may not always be an option. You may just need to learn to shoot even though you are experiencing double vision, or some other problem.

Finally, I have seen quite a few circumstances where the barricade is not considered part of the shooting area, and the shooter incurs penalties for touching it. I have even seen a couple stages where people end up zeroing the stage because of incidental contact with the barricade (not intentionally using it for support). Regardless of your opinion of what the correct interpretation of the rules are, I think everyone would agree it would be easiest just to avoid the issue altogether and not touch the barricade. Be sure you keep this in mind as you practice, and make sure you aren't touching the barricade if you don't intend to be.

Variations:

Be sure to try shooting this exercise while actually hanging on to the barricade or wall with your non-firing hand. You will need to stabilize your prop in order for it to work, but if you do things properly, you can practice one-handed shooting while you are supporting yourself on a structure. Sometimes stages require this; other times it will just open up an additional tactical option for you. Either way, you want to be proficient.

One-Handed Pickup

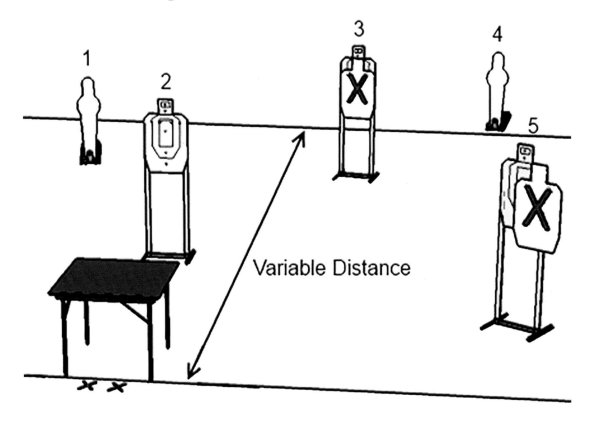

Variable Distance

Date:	Par Time:	Notes:
	NA	
	NA	
	NA	
	NA	
	NA	
	NA	
	NA	
	NA	
	NA	
	NA	

Variable Setup:

This is a "variable setup" drill. I outline a concept for a drill, and then you can construct it based on your own situation. Do not attempt to recreate the diagram. You should create the scenario outlined in the setup notes. The "How to Use This Book" section has more information on variable setups.

Setup Notes:

Aside from the usual assortment of targets, this exercise will require a table, barrel, or some other object to pick your pistol up from.

Procedure:

Start with both hands grasping the table. Pick your gun up using only your firing hand and engage the targets. Alternate between using your strong hand and your weak hand as your firing hand. **Continue to grasp the table with your non-firing hand.**

Focus:

You need to be able to establish a grip using only one hand to pick the pistol up.

Goal:

To consistently nail your grip and hit any required shot.

Commentary:

The whole challenge here is to be able to get a grip on your pistol with only one hand. I would perhaps deemphasize sheer speed in favor of ending up with a grip as near to perfect as you possibly can.

One thing you may want to try is getting your hand on the gun and lifting it up just a bit. You can then brace the gun on the table and get to your perfect grip. When you are picking the gun up, make sure you keep your finger well out of the trigger guard, so you don't put a round through the table.

Mover

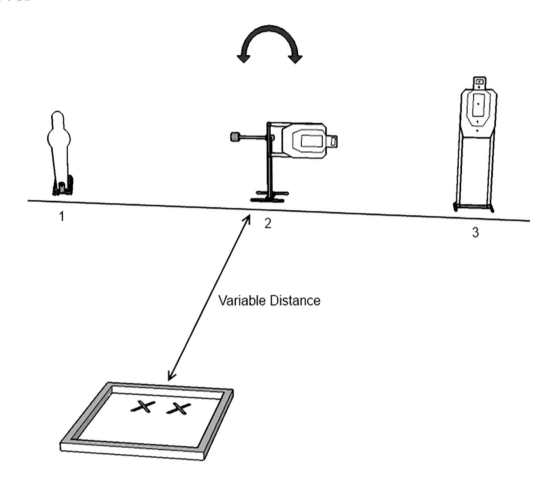

Variable Distance

Date:	Par Time:	Notes:
	NA	
	NA	
	NA	
	NA	
	NA	
	NA	
	NA	
	NA	
	NA	
	NA	

Variable Setup:

This is a "variable setup" drill. I outline a concept for a drill, and then you can construct it based on your own situation. Do not attempt to recreate the diagram. You should create the scenario outlined in the setup notes. The "How to Use This Book" section has more information on variable setups.

Setup Notes:

This drill will require some sort of moving target. A "swinger" is a good place to start, but you can certainly use anything you would like. There are more exotic moving targets, but you can learn the skills required by working on the more commonly available swingers.

If you use a swinger, it is a good habit to use a vision barrier to hide the moving target while it is at rest.

To round out the setup, place a static target near your moving target.

Set things up so you have a popper to activate your moving target.

The intent here is to have a "normal" speed moving target with a "normal" speed activator. If you have seen a few swingers in matches, you will have a good concept of what this should look like, and how to create it.

Procedure:

Engage the popper, then engage the static target, then engage the moving target.

Focus:

This is a beginner-level drill for getting comfortable with moving targets.

Goal:

To be able to consistently engage the static target after activation of the mover, and then to engage the mover (both shots on the first swing, if it is a swinger). There should be no sensation of rushing or being pushed to achieve this.

Commentary:

In order to compete at the higher levels of the sport, you are going to have to get used to the idea of activating a moving target, doing something else, and then engaging the mover. This drill is designed to help you learn that rudimentary prop timing. If you aren't yet in B class or above, you may want to skip this drill for now and work on something else. If you are in B class, it means you should be quick enough to make this work.

The core of this drill is to experience that you are indeed fast enough to shoot a target while the swinger moves into view and still have time to get the swinger on the first pass. So many shooters watch a prop activation during the walkthrough and decide that they aren't fast enough. It really isn't as tough as it looks; you just need to try it.

One of the biggest challenges here is that you will see the activator popper falling, and the moving target start its operation out of the corner of your eye. You need to learn to battle that distraction and execute the shots as planned. It is a very normal temptation to want to rush to get to the swinger, but it will frequently cause you to pick up some penalties. You need to get used to seeing the swinger moving and know that you will have time to get there regardless.

The above comments are mainly directed at using a swinger as your moving target. Other types of movers will present similar challenges. Try to expose yourself to as many different types as you can.

Variations:

After you are consistently able to get solid hits on all the targets, you can move to pushing your limits. You may want to require yourself to get three, four, or even more hits on the static target before you push over to the swinger. This will require just a bit more time and will perhaps induce a bit more rushing. Don't hesitate to increase the number of hits required to create more of a challenge for yourself if you think you need it.

Mover Sequence

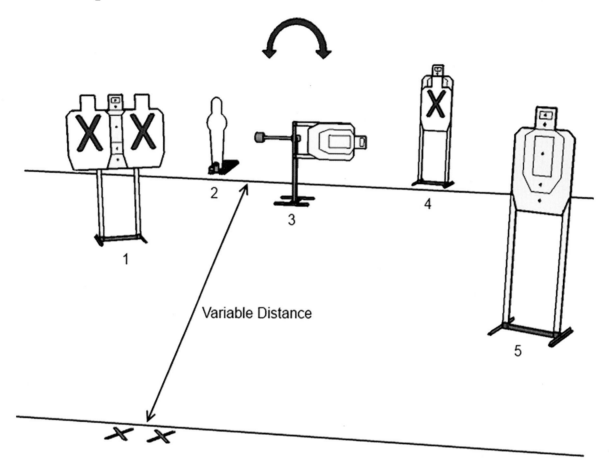

Variable Distance

Date:	Par Time:	Notes:
	NA	
	NA	
	NA	
	NA	
	NA	
	NA	
	NA	
	NA	
	NA	
	NA	

Variable Setup:

This is a "variable setup" drill. I outline a concept for a drill, and then you can construct it based on your own situation. Do not attempt to recreate the diagram. You should create the scenario outlined in the setup notes. The "How to Use This Book" section has more information on variable setups.

Setup Notes:

This drill will require some sort of moving target. A "swinger" or "drop turner" is a good place to start, but you can certainly use anything you would like. It should be a simple matter to at least locate a drop turner or swinger. There are more exotic moving targets, but you can learn the skills required by working on the more commonly available targets.

If you use a swinger, it is a good habit to use a vision barrier to hide the moving target while it is at rest.

Place targets of varying degrees of difficulty to the left and right of the activator and mover. You want to create a scenario that is complex, with a multitude of tactical options.

Set things up so you have a popper to activate your moving target.

The intent here is to have a "normal" speed moving target with a "normal" speed activator. If you have seen a few swingers in matches, you will have a good concept of what this should look like, and how to create it.

Procedure:

Start with your hands relaxed at sides. Engage all the targets in any order desired, but be sure you hit the moving target in an efficient fashion. You don't want to burn time waiting on it.

Focus:

To be able to come up with an efficient plan to engage a moving target and execute it consistently.

Goal:

You want to be able to identify and execute the best possible stage plan on your first attempt.

Commentary:

You can think of this little practice stage as your test lab for your moving target shooting ability and for your stage planning. Pay particular attention to the goal for this drill. You want your *first* attempt to be a well-executed run of the optimal stage plan for you at this moment in your development. That means that you will need to try other stage plans to confirm that you indeed chose the best plan during your first attempt. All of this means paying careful attention to the timer during your runs.

It is frequently the case during matches that you will see a moving target and have a few options for how to go about engaging it. You need to be able to come up with a good plan and nail the execution. Most shooters gain this experience not on a practice range, but during matches. If you aren't interested in learning the slow and expensive way, then you should set up these scenarios and work on them during your training.

I really like to emphasize wringing every last tenth of a second out of the stage time during my training on a little stage like this. That means not only aggressive shooting, but a really confident plan. It may be fastest to take a difficult target after the activator, but before the mover. This means you really need to be disciplined to make those shots and not rush. It is one thing to hit a 7-yard "burner" target after activating a swinger, but it is another matter entirely to take two carefully aimed shots at a 15-yard head box. You need to develop the discipline in practice so you can confidently shoot the best stage plan in a match situation without thinking you need to rush to make it happen.

Skipping Targets

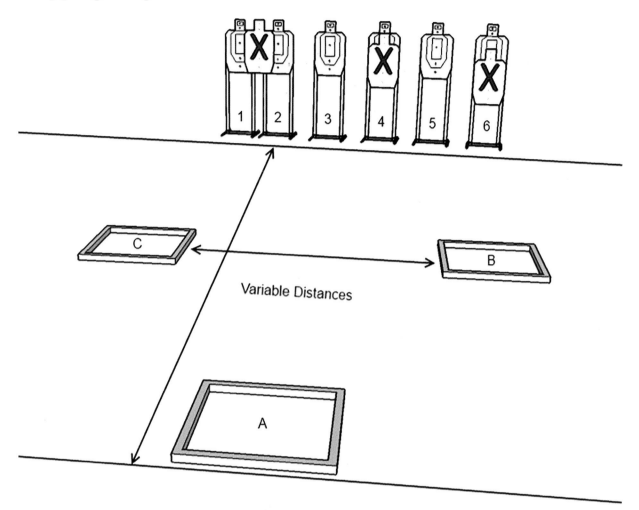

Date:	Par Time:	Notes:
	NA	
	NA	
	NA	
	NA	
	NA	
	NA	
	NA	
	NA	
	NA	
	NA	

Variable Setup:

This is a "variable setup" drill. I outline a concept for a drill, and then you can construct it based on your own situation. Do not attempt to recreate the diagram. You should create the scenario outlined in the setup notes. The "How to Use This Book" section has more information on variable setups.

Setup Notes:

This drill requires a line of six targets and three shooting positions, just like the diagram shows. It isn't really important how you arrange the no-shoots on the targets, but I do recommend that you use a few.

Procedure:

For this drill, the whole point is to pick a few targets to engage from each position, then remember that plan and execute it. The whole point is to be able to remember a complicated target engagement sequence, so I recommend you choose a complicated order.

For example, you could shoot Targets 1 and 6 from Position A, Targets 3 and 5 from Position B, then Targets 2 and 4 from Position C.

Frequently change the target engagement order.

Focus:

The idea here is to become comfortable with complicated target engagement sequences. You want to be able to cross targets with your gun and not shoot them.

Goal:

Execute a complicated engagement sequence with zero hesitation.

Commentary:

It is common at major matches that you will need to execute a stage plan that requires you to see a target, but skip shooting the target at that time, and then pick it up later on in the stage. People often end up engaging targets twice, or need to visually check a target to see if they engaged it, or they just end up hesitating trying to remember their plan. This drill is a good opportunity to work on those sorts of situations.

This drill works best if you have a training partner with you on the range. They can tell you what targets to engage from what position, give you 15 seconds to get ready, and then give you the start signal. This way produces some pressure. It helps force you to make some mistakes. This is a positive thing; you want to make those mistakes in practice, not at a match. You will never be put in a situation at a match where you need to program in a stage plan, and then execute it 15 seconds later. This will probably help you feel like matches are actually a lot easier.

One thing I like to do is to use markers on the stage to help me remember things. I might want to engage every target to the left of the barrel stack from one position, and then just shoot everything I can see from another position. Depending on how you set this one up, you may be able to use similar markers. Shooting all the partial targets from one spot, and then all the other targets from another, or something of that nature. In any event, figure out a way to remember what you need to remember, and then get after it.

Variations:

One fun variation you can do is to take a six-sided die and roll it a few times for every position. You will end up with a lot of numbers, and then engage the appropriate target number from the appropriate position.

Chapter 8
DESIGNING PRACTICE STAGES

Sometimes it is a good idea to set up a full-on stage for practice. This isn't something that you should do every time you shoot, but it is a good idea, occasionally. There is a certain amount of experience you get from working through a more complicated stage, as opposed to a simple practice drill. You need to learn to flow through a longer set of different challenges, as opposed to working on just one skill at a time. If you don't go to many club level matches, then getting some trigger time on stages that you build yourself is not a bad idea.

Before we get too deep into this, I want to caution you about working on practice stages. This is a good way to work on flowing through a stage and figuring out a stage, but not really the most efficient way to develop specific skills. You are going to be burning through a lot of time and ammunition every time you shoot a stage, so remember that this isn't really the way to get better at the little details of your shooting. If you go overboard with this, you may well be wasting resources that are better spent elsewhere. Stage practice should be a very occasional thing, not a regular occurrence.

In any event, a well-designed practice stage should combine a few different skills together into a longer and more complicated stage. I don't know that it is beneficial to create a full-on 32-round stage for your own shooting, but a smaller 12-20 round deal can be extremely productive. You want to have just enough rounds to make the stage such that you can run around a little bit and work on some complicated challenges, but there isn't really any reason to go beyond that. Save the ammo and stay away from massive practice stages.

Another important thing you can learn with stage practice is how to break stages down properly. If you have questions about whether it's better to go left, then go right. Really, for any of a million different questions people have about stages, you can get some answers by experimenting on a big stage. Again, it is more efficient to do this on the smaller scenarios included previously in this book, but you can glean some good information from larger stages.

The key thing to understand here is that if you design a little practice stage, there is no limit to the skill sets you can work on. You can pull elements from any of the preceding drills and exercises and mix them together in ways that you haven't seen before. You can blend them in ways that have given you trouble in matches. You can try new things in the practice laboratory without fear of any negative consequences.

The process for setting up these practice stages is really simple:

1. Pick a set of elements you want to work on.
2. Construct a stage that combines those elements.
3. Come up with the rules of the stage.

The meaning of all of the above steps should be self-evident, except perhaps for number 3. By "rules," I mean you should decide which targets must be engaged from what position, and so on. Since you probably don't have time to construct a full-on stage with all the wall sections that would normally be required, you are going to have to settle for stipulating where each target gets engaged from. You might say "this target needs to be engaged from the left side of this wall," or "this target can be shot from anywhere it is visible." No matter what you come up with, you will need to have some rules that you are going to force yourself to follow as you shoot the stage.

Keep in mind as you come up with these rules that you can decide to engage one target multiple times over the course of the stage; this saves you some setup time for additional targets. One caution here is that it may be more difficult to determine where problems are occurring on that target if you engage it multiple times, because you will have to figure out from which position a poor shot was fired.

I will provide you with a couple sample stages so you can get an idea of how this works.

Sample Stage 1

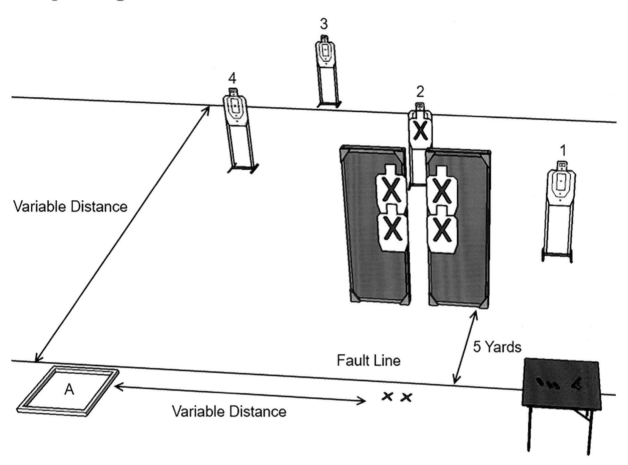

Date:	Par Time:	Notes:
	NA	
	NA	
	NA	
	NA	
	NA	
	NA	
	NA	
	NA	
	NA	
	NA	

Elements used:

Narrow port
Table
Partial targets
Distant targets
Short distance movement

Rules:

Start in Position A. Retrieve your gun from the table, and engage each target with two rounds. Targets 2 and 3 must be engaged through the narrow port. Targets 1 and 4 may be engaged from anywhere, as long as it is uprange of the fault line. Move to Box A and engage each target with an additional two rounds.

Variations:

Require all magazines to start on the table.
Require the gun to start unloaded.
Require the stage to be shot strong hand only.
Require the first eight shots to be fired while the shooter is moving.

Sample Stage 2

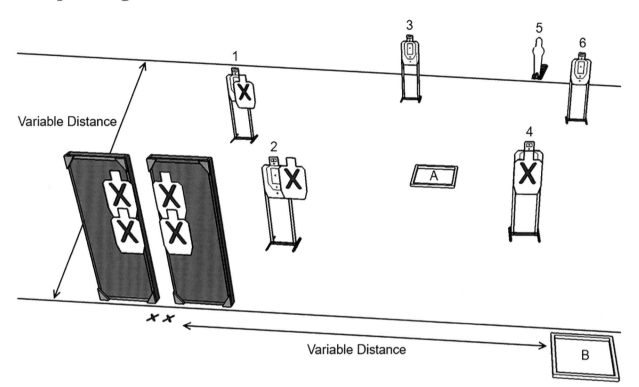

Date:	Par Time:	Notes:
	NA	
	NA	
	NA	
	NA	
	NA	
	NA	
	NA	
	NA	
	NA	
	NA	

Elements Used:

Partial targets

Poppers

Narrow port

Long distance movement

Distance transitions

Rules:

Start in Position B with your hands relaxed at sides. Targets 1 and 2 must be shot through the port. The popper must be shot from Position A. Target 4 must be shot from Position B. Other targets can be shot from any desired location.

Variations:

Start at the port.

Start in Position A.

Require the stage be shot one-handed.

Chapter 9
DESIGNING YOUR TRAINING PLAN

If you have looked over the drills, you may have a lot of questions.

- What drills do I do first?
- How much do I do them?
- What drills are more important?
- What drills did you do to get good?

All of these (and more) are valid questions. All the drills in the world aren't going to make any difference if you can't get organized and attack them in some systematic way. The point of this section is to give you the tools to make that happen.

Now, many people would simply want me to give them "The Plan," so they can follow it. The issue is, absolutely no two people are alike, and so it seems to me that not everyone should use the same plan. People have different skills, different strengths and weaknesses, different equipment, different resources, and so on.

Thus, I will not be giving you "The Plan." You will need to use the tools you have, and use your own intellect to formulate your own plan. Granted, the system in this book is detailed, and it shouldn't be difficult to do, but in honesty, you simply must do it for yourself. There is only so much I can do for you.

Designing Your Training Plan
As far as I am concerned, the process is very straightforward. However, it can get a little bit complicated. I will outline it for you and then get into some detail.

First, you figure out where you want to go in terms of skill. Do you want to be winning your club matches? Do you want to be a certain classification? Do you want to be competitive at the section match level? What is it you want to get out of the sport?

Next, you figure out where you are. You need to know where your skills stand in the greater scheme of things. You need to know what your relative strengths and weaknesses are. If you don't know what you are good at and what you are bad at, then it is tough to have an effective plan to address these things.

The Dream
Every plan to get better needs to start with a goal. Do you want to be pretty good? Do you want to be state champion? Maybe you just don't want to embarrass yourself on the range. In any event, having a desire to get better is where it starts.

Fortunately, I can't imagine someone without a desire to get better even bothering to read this book. Desire is a self-regulating issue for the most part. I must say, I don't often deal with people that lack desire to improve. I am not on the local shooting scene much, but people that attend my classes or major matches tend to be serious about improvement. This isn't to say that everyone is hell-bent on world domination; this is saying that people want to improve.

I think it is important to want to be better, and to be open about it. It may piss people off that you want to get better. Too bad for them. I remember one infamous incident where a top shooter stated on a forum that he didn't shoot a lot of local matches because there wasn't much competition for him there. He provoked some genuine resentment by saying that, and ended up departing the forum. The fact is, if you decide you want to get better, you shouldn't be ashamed of it. Some guys will talk shit about you behind your back. People may make fun of you for failing to achieve whatever goal you set for yourself. You will have to harden up and deal with it.

Whatever your goal, you can't be afraid of it. Winning your club matches is within your reach. Guys that you think are "untouchable" are humans, not gods. It will take some work, but there is no reason you can't learn to shoot like a champion.

Specific Goals

Having a general goal is great, but without some sort of specifics, a general goal is just a vague ambition.

For example, if you want to win your section match, then what is it going to take to do that? If the winner the previous few years has been a solid A class shooter, then you know that if you become a solid M class shooter, you will have a good chance at winning the match. That isn't a specific enough goal, though.

Picking what class you want to be is a great start, but there is so much more you can do.

How tight of a slow fire group do you need to be able to shoot?

How fast does your draw need to be?

How fast should you be able to reload?

Etc.

Of course, any of the above questions would need to be followed up with some sort of stipulations. If we are talking about group shooting, then it is X gun at X distance with X ammunition using X target. This stuff gets complicated in a big hurry!

In order to help you with some specific goals, I am going to give you a few things you should think about. Just bear in mind, as you start talking about more and more complicated skills, it becomes nearly impossible to accurately get a measurement outside of a match situation. It is one of those things that requires a very experienced eye. If someone is a very good shooter, it may take me quite a bit of observation in a class setting to figure out where they need to go with their training. It can be complicated, especially for the field course drills where you don't have a specific performance standard to can work from.

First, we can talk about classification goals. I am not going to bother with anything lower than B class, because if you train regularly, you don't have any business in C or D.

B class is tricky for a few reasons. It is the classification that encompasses a wide variety of skill levels. There are people in B class that have misses on nearly every stage of a club match. There are IDPA Masters. There are people that can shoot great groups. There are Master-level bullseye shooters. There are brand-new shooters that have only owned a pistol for six months, then went out and shot their way into B class. As you can see, there are a lot of ways to get into B!

The reason there is such a broad array of skill levels in that class is that the classification system works by testing your ability to draw quickly, reload quickly, and shoot reasonably accurate at medium range targets. If you can shoot something like four shots a second into 10-yard targets with 75 percent "A" hits, you will likely end up in B class. If you are super accurate, but super slow, it may seem tough to get into B class.

The following is the standard exercise quick reference times adjusted for a goal of being in B class. All the 50-yard stuff is omitted, because it just isn't needed.

If you can consistently put down these times in practice, with all "A"s or close "C"s, I simply can't imagine you not being at least in B class. If you compare this chart to the chart I gave for people looking to be GMs, then you will see there is a bit of time added to everything, but a bit *more* time added for the longer distance drills. The reasoning behind that is that lower-classed shooters can get away with a slower draw and reload time across the board. Also, spending more time aiming at the longer shots is common in the lower classes. At longer ranges, the focus for people looking to get to B class should be to make the hits. I have backed off on the times to emphasize that point.

Distance	3 yards	5 yards	7 yards	10 yards	15 yards	20 yards	25 yards
Doubles	1.3	1.4	1.5	1.6	1.8	2.0	2.5
Bill Drill	2.0	2.2	2.5	2.7	3.0	4.0	5.0
Blake Drill	NA	2.2	2.5	2.8	3.5	NA	NA
Singles	1.5	1.7	1.9	2.1	2.5	3.0	3.5
El Prez	NA	NA	6.0	6.5	7.5	NA	12
Four Aces	3.0	3.2	3.5	4.0	4.5	5.0	5.5
SHO	3.0	3.5	4.0	4.5	5.0	6.5	8.0
WHO	4.0	4.5	5.0	6.0	6.5	7.0	10
Bill/Reload	5.0	5.5	6.0	6.5	7.0	9.0	11
Heads	NA	4.0	4.5	5.0	6.0	NA	8.0
Crisscross	NA	8.0	8.5	9.0	10	11	NA

If you are already at the B class or A class level, and are looking to move up, you should be working from the charts in the standard exercises section. Not every shooter will be able to make every single par time, but you can systematically work through the drills and try to get up to speed on that skill. You need to couple this with regular dryfire training, placing a particular focus on draw speed and reload speed.

Match Analysis

If you are in a situation where you are already M or GM, then it becomes more challenging to choose some specific goals. In my opinion, if you want to get better at that point, I think you need to go out and get your ass kicked at some major matches. With only a modicum of intelligence, you should be able to diagnose what you could do better in a match. Many people do a good deal of self-analysis already, but I want to give you a few ideas that should help you improve.

In my opinion, the key to having a good training plan for a shooter that already has good fundamentals is properly analyzing major match results. Once you know what you need to get better at, it should be easy to go back through this book and locate the appropriate drill to take to the range. However, there are some common problems with this process. I think it is super important, after looking at your major match scores, to differentiate between mistakes, systemic issues, stage tactics, technique, and match percentage.

Mistakes

First, right up front, you need to understand that everyone makes mistakes. No matter how good you are, you will, on occasion, screw things up. I think this is extremely important to point out for a number of reasons.

If you are analyzing match results, and you made a particularly boneheaded mistake on a stage that cost you a lot, then it is tempting to want to do something to "fix" yourself so that it doesn't happen again. However, no matter how much you train, you may still

occasionally make a similar mistake. If, for example, you screw up a draw on a stage and miss your grip, you may be tempted to "fix" that problem. However, if you are already doing 30 minutes a day of dryfire, I don't really see how increasing your practice is going to fix the problem. By focusing on a one-time mistake that you made, you are actually holding back your training. You could well work on some other area of your shooting and improve your match score a lot more than dumping more effort into a skill that you already spend a lot of time on.

You should also recognize that other shooters make mistakes. If there is a particular shooter that you compare your scores to on a regular basis, you shouldn't read too much into a stage where they made a mistake and it affected the results. For example, if you have been working hard on shooting while moving, and then there is a stage that emphasizes that skill, you would want to pay careful attention to those stage results. However, if your competitor had a miss and a no-shoot hit on the stage, and it swung the results your way, you wouldn't necessarily want to conclude too much from the fact you beat them on the stage. The point is, shooters tend to read too much into stage results. Just as you have ups and downs, so will other people.

Systemic Issues

When you are analyzing match results, it is helpful to look for issues that present themselves on a regular basis. Essentially, you need to look through the regular ups and downs that everyone has at a match and see where you need to go with your training. Screwing up one "strong hand" stage isn't a big deal. Being unable to effectively do any strong hand stage is an issue you are going to need to correct through some training. It is important to recognize the difference.

With good match analysis, you are looking to recognize systemic problems in your shooting. What skills do you actually need to work on?

As your understanding of the sport grows, your understanding of stage results will grow. You can't recognize systemic issues if you don't understand what a stage is "about." There is more to shooting than just "speed" and "accuracy." As you have seen at this point, there is a whole litany of specific skills that you can work on. You need to match up those specific skills to the stages you are shooting. You need to know what fits where, so to speak. Don't think, "Oh I need to go faster," get more specific. Do you need to work on position entry drills? Are you having an issue getting your reload done before you get to a new position? Identify the things that are costing you time and work to improve them.

The same process is in play when you are looking at things you do well. If you are a fantastic distance shooter, then you should be able to identify that it needs to be de-emphasized in your training. It is commonly understood that people prefer to practice what they are already good at. Don't be that person. Pat yourself on the back about the things you are good at, but remember it will actually hurt your shooting to keep practicing the stuff that you don't need to work at.

Stage Tactics

By "stage tactics," I mean the decisions you make on a stage during the walkthrough process. This is also known as "stage breakdown," "stage doping," or "stage diagnosis" (among other things).

Stage tactics are undoubtedly part of the game. At any major match, you can bet the top shooters will be there the day before, figuring out the most efficient ways to shoot the stages, and deciding on their tactics. I spend an average of two hours on site at a major match the day before I actually shoot. That time is spent on figuring out the best path through the stages and memorizing the layout.

One of the best learning opportunities at a major match is seeing how other people shoot the stages. There is always a bit of variation among the top shooters in terms of how they approach various stages. As far as sorting out the "best" way, it is extremely difficult. If you pay attention at every match you go to, and pay attention during your training, you will improve it very quickly.

The point I want to make here is that, as important as stage tactics are in determining your score, many people will overvalue them. For example, if you have a choice of going right or going left, don't assume that going left is the best because the person that won the stage went left. Don't assume that one way is better than the other way. Don't attribute some deficiency in your own score to your stage plan, unless you are certain you did things "wrong."

The bottom line here is that while stage tactics are an interesting and valuable subject, your score is primarily going to be execution driven. Put another way, a crappy plan executed well can win you a stage.

What you should do is pay attention to the choices other shooters make on stages, and try to determine why they made that choice. Why did Zack shoot the stage that way? Was there an advantage? Try and figure it out! Get interested in it. But, understand that it usually isn't going to make or break your match.

Technique
Technique is the "how" behind the "what." This is a complicated issue! I could write a whole book about handgun technique (I actually already did).

With such a broad topic, it is important that you always pay attention, and look to do things better. Maybe you want to change your draw stroke technique from a "press out" draw to an "index" draw. In any event, if you decide to make a technical change, you should understand that it will take some serious work to actually implement that change, and have it happen subconsciously.

Another important thing you should do is understand the effect that technique has on your shooting. Working on little details like hand position during your draw is not something that is going to take you from D class to A class. It just doesn't work that way. Little technical details will net you almost imperceptible gains. On the other hand, making a big change in your approach will net a big change in your score.

You should constantly and carefully evaluate your shooting technique. Things change over time. You should evaluate your game to make sure you are doing things the best way possible.

One other note here: you may think that you are doing things a certain way, but then if you see footage of yourself, you will notice that you aren't actually doing things the way you think you are doing them. The important thing here is that people can be taught one way, and they "buy in" to that way (think it is best), they train to do things that way, and then still do not actually execute that technique at matches. If you aren't paying attention, you will not realize that things aren't working the way you think they are.

Match Percentage
This advice may fly in the face of common practice at USPSA events, but I recommend you be extremely careful when using the match percentages as an indicator of much of anything. Finishing 98 percent of some guy at one match may or may not bear any relationship to finishing 85 percent of some other guy at some other match.

Of course, you can get a good general idea of a number of factors. You can see who beat whom, and by approximately how much, but beyond that you should exercise great care.

First, every match is different. It seems obvious, but it bears mention. Different stages, with a different competitive field, makes for entirely different match percentages. Having a match of relatively easy stages can bunch everyone up in terms of percentages. Having lots of really difficult stages tends to spread people out. Having a small number of shooters competing with each other tends to make it possible for people to be widely spread. There are many variables here. It is complicated!

The really important thing to remember with match percentages is that one stage can swing the percentages in a big way. One bad stage from the match winner, or spectacular stage from you (or maybe both), will impact the final percentages meaningfully.

The bottom line: don't read too much into the percentages.

Skills Inventory

In order to figure out where you want to go, you need to figure out where you are. What I mean by this is that you need to have a detailed idea of where you stand as a shooter. Many people can make general statements about their shooting ability. You might hear someone say, "I am in B class." Someone might say, "I am accurate, but I am slow." Statements like that may well be true, but to effectively design a training plan for yourself, you are going to need a lot more detailed information.

It is best if you can break down your ability with as many quantifiable numbers as possible. It is best if you understand how different circumstances affect those numbers. For example, you can hit a 0.90 draw with your hands relaxed at sides at seven yards about 75 percent of the time under practice conditions. What about 10 yards? What about a partial target? What about 13 yards? What about a turning draw? What do the times actually look like in matches?

Surely you can see that all of this stuff gets complicated in a big hurry. There is a lot

more data you can collect and learn from than thinking of yourself as a B class shooter. Just about everything can be quantified, calculated, and distilled down to the point where you can see exactly how good you are at certain skills, and how you should get better.

Earlier in the book, I am sure you noticed I had five sections filled with drills to help you improve your skill levels. These areas were marksmanship drills, transition drills, standard exercises, movement skills, and other skills.

In keeping with this organization pattern, I will propose a detailed scheme to help you inventory your own skills.

Of course, I don't want to discount match analysis. That is obviously an important consideration when formulating your training plan, but I strongly feel that it is important to do more than just match analysis. You can test the skills that are important for you to test on your own time, in your own way, away from a match environment. In a match, you don't usually get the opportunity to make detailed measurements of target distances, or to take a look at all the split times that the timer records. Matches give you an aggregate picture of where you stand, but more detailed information can give you a better picture of where you need to go with your training.

Marksmanship Drills

Marksmanship drills can easily be assessed by simply shooting the drills. The distances and targets are defined quite clearly and there shouldn't be confusion about the standards. I strongly recommend that you use "Practical

Accuracy" as a benchmark drill to assess your shooting ability.

You should also pay attention during matches to make sure that you feel (in a subjective sense) that you are able to make every shot that you are presented with. If you feel you can't make the shots in a match situation, it destroys confidence. You need to address that situation during your training.

Transition Drills

Transition drills lack any objective standard, so that makes it quite difficult to benchmark yourself. I recommend that you calculate hit factors if you are in doubt about your transition ability. On any given drill, your first run should be within 20 percent of your best run. This is a good test because it forces you to at least be competent on your first run and not practice and get better during your subsequent runs.

Standard Exercises

Standard exercises are primarily something to work on if you are looking to increase your classification or confirm that your static shooting skills are up to par. The assortment of drills in this book are a very good test and shooters all around the competitive shooting community shoot them and work on them regularly.

Movement Skills

Testing your movement skills can be a little bit complicated. You want to have more information other than knowing if you are "good" or "bad." You need some way to measure your progress in less simplistic terms.

The way I have always done this is to identify certain types of stages. There are stages with a lot of rounds fired and a lot of movement. There are stages that are stand and shoot affairs (like classifiers). There are stages that are very prop driven, with tons of moving targets. There are all kinds of stages.

What you need to do is identify the "run and gun" type of stages at the matches you attend. You can get a sense of where you stand compared to other shooters that attend those same matches. I recommend that you keep a close eye on shooters that are consistent performers, not necessarily the best. You can track your stage times against the consistent performers that you have identified. Over time, you will get a sense of where you stand, and whether you are improving or not.

Other Skills

You can test your other skills in a similar fashion to the movement skills; that is to say, you are going to compare your performance to a selection of consistent performers that you shoot against regularly. However, I recommend that you add in a bit of subjectivity. You should think about how prepared you feel when you encounter the oddball elements in the sport that I addressed in the other skills section.

If you encounter prone shooting, and you feel like you shot terribly and left a lot on the table, then you should remember to train more on that. Other shooters may have also done poorly, so you may not have done poorly in a comparative sense. However, you know that you could have done much better. I think this subjective element is important, because relatively few shooters put in the time or effort to be truly well-rounded competitors.

Running the Drills

I think I should point out that you have some important options in terms of how you want to run the benchmark drills. As I see it, you should run the drills in a consistent fashion in order to get accurate benchmarks. For example, you may want to run your benchmarks at the beginning of a practice session and get a "cold" set of numbers. You may want to run them "warmed up," and take a measurement that way. There are advantages and disadvantages to both ways, but the key is to have a consistent system for how you are going to measure yourself.

Mental Game

It seems logical to want to assess the shape of your "mental game." You absolutely can do this during your own training, but the measurement is going to be subjective. You need to create the sensation of match pressure in your training environment. You can do this by having someone you respect watch you shoot. You can remind yourself of how much work you put into the sport in order to spur some pressure. You can compare your current ability to your past ability and see if that puts some pressure on you.

Once you are feeling pressure during your training, you can shoot a few exercises or practice stages, and see if that pressure causes you to fall apart or not.

Of course, you should also pay attention to your pressure situation during matches to see if your mental management is improving. If you want to win big matches, you are going to need to learn to perform under pressure.

Designing Your Plan

You may well be intimidated at the sheer volume of ideas, methods, and drills that are contained in this book. Questions like "What drill do I start with?" and "How many times should I practice each week?" are extremely common. This section is designed to help you formulate your own plan or strategy.

These sorts of things are some of the more common questions I get from people. How many times a week should I practice? How many rounds should I fire? How much dryfire should I do? I have even had shooters ask me to give them a training plan as detailed as how many repetitions of each drill to do. Frankly, I think planning things at that level of detail is unnecessary. More to the point, I can't give you that plan. You need to be the master of your own plan in order to be completely effective.

Choose Your Level of Involvement

I think one of the most important things you can do as a shooter is to make a decision about how involved in the sport you want to be. Do you see yourself just shooting club matches? Do you want to shoot a couple state level matches each year? Maybe you want to do well at nationals. In any event, I think it is important to figure that out early on.

You should also figure out how much you are willing to put into training for the sport.

Are you going to practice once a week? Are you willing to dryfire every day?

The reason I point this out is that you don't want to have a disconnect between your level of involvement and your expectations. I see people all the time that are frustrated to the point of quitting, but at the same time their expectations are totally out of sync with their practice level. To be blunt, you can't really expect to beat people that work at shooting if you don't take shooting that seriously.

Have a Goal

Having a goal is important. It helps you direct your efforts in a positive direction rather than simply trying hard. A good goal is something that is measurable. You should be able to know whether or not you were successful. Of course, this may sound obvious, but you might be surprised how many people have "goals" that sound more like a vague ambition than a quantifiable achievement. This is about getting to B class vs. getting "better."

It is usually best to select a goal that isn't dependent on what other people do. If you have a goal to win some specific match, you may well have some other motivated individuals come and have the match of their life and beat you. That doesn't mean that you are a failure, it just means that the other person had a great day. It is often better to select a goal that you can control the outcome of. Trying to shoot an entire match without any penalties is a great goal, and it doesn't in any way depend on what someone else is doing.

You don't just need to have goals in a match situation, you can benefit from them in practice as well. This is the reason I have included a goal for every single drill contained in this book. Some of them are extremely specific, others are a bit more general. In any case, having a goal is what turns a trip to the range into a training session. The goal can help you direct your energy, and help you get focused.

The point here is that just like you want to have goals for practice sessions, you want to have larger, more long-term goals for your training, generally. Saying, "I want to master these three specific drills in the next six weeks," for example, is a way to have you working toward something rather than just working.

Resources

Carefully examining your available resources is absolutely critical to crafting a realistic and appropriate goal. The whole idea is to figure out what you have available to you and budget it appropriately. This isn't just about money; this is about all the things that will be required to be successful in competition.

You may need to have some difficult conversations with your family (usually your spouse) about how you plan to spend your time and money. You will almost certainly be taking time away from other obligations in order to accomplish your shooting goals. If you are unable to bring the amount of resources to bear on shooting that you think you will need, then you may want to consider setting a more appropriate goal.

This exercise is important. This isn't just about planning your season, it is about coming to grip with the reality of how much time and money your level of involvement is going to require. I have repeatedly seen people be really motivated to shoot at the beginning of the year, but after half a season, the bills start to pile up, and it becomes a problem for them. Budgeting early on is the best way to avoid any system shock you may experience later on.

Time

In my opinion, the most important thing at your disposal is your time. Training at a high level will require constant effort and a daily time commitment. You will need to dry-fire, livefire, load ammo, clean brass, maintain your guns, troubleshoot gear, plan for matches, and attend matches. There is a lot of work involved in all of this, and it can be time consuming.

With work and family obligations to consider, you are going to need to carefully budget your time.

Energy

If you want to go beyond simply participating, then you are going to have to put forward some effort. This means more than just getting off the couch to practice. This means you need to do more than just go through the motions of practice. You need to invest actual mental energy in your training.

Money

Shooting isn't exactly a rich man's game, but it isn't cheap either. You will need to pay for guns, ammunition, range access, travel expenses, and so on. If you aren't willing to throw down the cash, then it will be tough to get really good at the sport. This isn't to say that you need loads of money to do well. A few hundred dollars a month (on average) can be enough to make you a very solid GM shooter.

Priorities

When it comes down to it, you need to make shooting your priority if you want to be really good at it. I see people all the time that get really heavily into shooting for two months at a time, then they disappear. Maybe they go pursue some other hobby for a while, or they are just taking a break from shooting. Everyone knows that person, and they frequently don't really make much improvement. If you are serious about shooting, then be serious about shooting.

Putting the Time In

After you take stock of your resources, you need to come up with a plan to schedule things. You absolutely must put in the time to get good. I have a few tips for you.

Practice Schedule

Ideally, you should practice on a regular basis. You don't want to be the guy that hits it hard for two months, and then doesn't do anything for six. If you have enough ammo for 300 rounds a week, then maybe you want to split that up into two sessions. You want to hit those sessions regularly, every week.

Now, you should adjust your practice schedule a bit based on your match schedule. You certainly should ramp up the number of sessions and the round count before an important match. I think doubling the amount of practice you do for a couple of weeks before a "goal" match is a helpful thing.

When it is your offseason, you should do little or no livefire practice. If you don't have a major match coming for six months, then don't think you need to keep up a heavy practice schedule. Slow things down a little bit.

Match Schedule

Your match schedule should be put together carefully. It is probably your goal to do well at major matches if you are reading this book. If not, I can't imagine how you made it this far in. If you shoot a couple section matches and an area match, it is likely you want to put on the best show at the area match. Your club match schedule should reflect all of this.

I find it helpful to shoot a club match or two before I go to a major match. This helps you experience some match pressure. It gives you an opportunity to break down stages and visualize your plan. It helps get you into that competition mode. For these reasons, you should schedule some less important matches to help you get ready for the more important matches.

On the other hand, you should be realistic about the matches you actually want to shoot. I don't recommend that you compete year-round, certainly. If you are shooting matches

as a social event, that is fine, but recognize that it may be a waste of time from a training perspective, or at least unproductive in the larger scheme of improving your shooting. I have seen some people slow their training down during the offseason but continue to shoot club matches. Of course, they don't do as well as they would like, so it actually causes them to get frustrated and demoralized. Really, they are out there competing when they have put themselves in a position where they can't do their best.

The solution to all of this is to have a match schedule that emphasizes preparing you for your important matches and gives you a breather during the slow season.

Avoiding Burnout

I want to reemphasize the importance of avoiding burnout. It is really important to give yourself an off-season. It is helpful to peak your training at the right times. You may be thinking, "why not train like a madman year-round?" The fact is, in every sport there is downtime. Nobody can go full steam year-round for years on end. You have a life outside of shooting. You probably have a family. You have others stuff you need to do. If you are in this sport for the long haul, then you are going to need to schedule your time wisely.

Personally, I have made mistakes in my scheduling where I am pushing too hard for six or eight weeks during the middle of the shooting season. I may have matches and classes lined up every single weekend for months on end. It doesn't help my shooting. Eventually,

I just need to take a week away from the range, and that isn't what you want to happen during the peak season. Don't make those mistakes. Don't push yourself to the point where you just can't keep your heart in it. You want to stay hungry. Stay motivated. You should always feel like you have the energy to go to the range and improve. You should feel refreshed and ready to compete, not beaten down and tired.

Reality Check for D and C Class Shooters

If you apply the concepts in this book, you will not be in D or C class for very long at all. Simply put, if you are still in C class a year after starting on the training program I have described, then you screwed up. The reality check here is that people come into the sport with bad fundamentals, no particular talent, the wrong equipment, and may still find a way to classify in B.

If you train seriously, then you have no place in C class.

Reality Check for M and GM Class Shooters

If you are a motivated and perhaps talented shooter, you will probably end up in M or GM class before too long. If you want to move beyond that and become a death-stalker on a national level, you will need more. You may have looked past some of the drills in this book thinking you have already mastered those skills. You may think that you have nothing more to learn in certain areas.

The fact is, the best shooters in the game are always working to improve. Even if you are one of the best in the world at some specific skill area, you can still learn through your training.

If you want to get better, you should systematically work your way through all of the drills and ideas contained in this book. Carefully read the commentary for the drills. Explore new ideas. Accept that you have a lot to learn. You need to take the M class ego and set it aside if you want to improve.

Chapter 10
DOCUMENTATION

At this point in the book, you are probably thinking that there are a whole plethora of things you want to try and want to do. It is probably a really intimidating thing when you get right down to it. There are so many things to try and do, and so many things to keep in your head at once that it may well be impossible to actually pull it off.

In my opinion, it actually is impossible to keep track of your training entirely in your head. You need to have some mechanism to keep tabs on what is going on. You need to have some idea of what your goals are, and to monitor your training in some way.

Range Diary
Keeping a range diary may not sound like something that a manly man does. It isn't what it sounds like. You just need some way to keep track of your shooting, as well as a way to keep you focused. Many shooters go with an online range diary format, and I don't think that is a bad idea. You have a place to compile information about when you are practicing, what drills you are shooting, what type of issues you are experiencing, and so on. You want to make a note of equipment issues as well, as malfunctions need to be taken seriously.

You don't need to keep your range diary publicly; many people opt not to. Keeping it out in the open may subject you to comments or interactions that you don't want to have. The important point here is that you have some record of what is happening with your shooting.

Video
With the ease of recording video, there isn't a good reason for you not to use it as a way to diagnose and catalog your shooting techniques and habits. You only need to have a smartphone, and you can get serviceable quality video. It is easy to upload that video to YouTube, and have it stored indefinitely. If you don't want to have the videos available publicly, adjust your privacy settings on your account accordingly.

Quite simply, there is no reason not to get video on a regular basis. Perhaps you don't need it every match, but it is a simple thing to get a bit of video. It is a valuable tool.

Match Scores
Scores from your matches are stored indefinitely on the USPSA site, and I recommend you keep tabs on them. At the end of the day, I suppose the whole point is to do well in matches, so there is no reason not to keep track.

One thing I will caution you about is to look for patterns over a series of matches. Don't get too wrapped up in one match, and certainly don't get wrapped up in one stage result. Look at the big picture. People have bad matches now and again, and you don't want a couple of mistakes made at a match to make you feel like a failure. On the flip side of that coin, you don't want to get complacent because you had a relatively good match.

Chapter 11
EFFICIENT PRACTICE SESSIONS

It is my firm belief that having a focused and efficient practice session is absolutely essential to your development as a shooter. Let me make this clear. I think that if you can accomplish a quality practice session in half an hour, as opposed to two hours, you ought to do it. I think it is reasonable to perhaps put less actual effort into the sport, but to get better than you ever were, as long as you are directing that effort in an intelligent way. If you take the time to have a *plan*, you can go out and accomplish your *goals*. When you have done what you set out to do, you can go home for the day. Of course, if you are really motivated, you can always work harder, but direct that work in a focused and productive way.

During the 2011 shooting season, I frequently would only have enough time for a 20- or 30-minute range session a few times a week. I had a ton of obligations outside of shooting, but I was still very serious about my shooting and my training. I had always been a believer in efficient practice, but during this year my beliefs were really tested. Could I spend only a couple hours a week (most weeks) on a shooting range for the balance of the year and still be ready for nationals?

The answer was yes.

I have done some serious study on the issue of practice efficiency over the last few years. I have even had students in classes set up and do a practice session, so I can observe what they are doing. Generally speaking, I can criticize their practice as slow, inefficient, unfocused, and aimless. That may sound like a harsh list of criticisms, but in my opinion, there is no avoiding the truth.

When you go out to practice, ask yourself the following questions:
What am I trying to accomplish?
How long should this be taking?
Am I wasting any time?

Have a Plan for Your Practice Session
In my opinion, an efficient practice session starts and ends with a plan. When you go out to the range, you should know what it is you are working on. If you go to the range with no idea what you are going to do, you are usually going to end up either working on the same old stuff that you always work on (practicing what you are already good at), or working on nothing (just random blasting). Having a plan is about more than just knowing what you are going to do that day, it is about having lots of well-planned practice days that fit into a plan to help you improve over the long term. A plan is about identifying the things you need to fix, and then working on all of them systematically.

Focused Drills

If you carefully read the goal and focus sections of all of the drills in this book, you should have a very clear understanding of what the drills are for. It is absolutely essential that you use focused drills to try and move your skill level forward. When you are out on the range, select the appropriate drills that help you improve. Your range session will be much more productive for having done that.

You are Accountable

At the end of the day, I encourage you to hold yourself accountable for what you do and how you do it. It is easy to blame family obligations, work, the weather, your gunsmith, or any number of other people for what you do. Yes, it is tough to push forward in shooting. Your results are on you. You need to bring an attitude to practice that what you are able to do in practice genuinely matters. You absolutely must demand ever higher levels of performance from yourself. That is why you have some sort of goal for every exercise in this book. The goal is there to help you push toward something.

A Few Practice Tips

I thought it might be helpful to give you some tips to help make your practice more efficient. These tips are in no particular order.

Have a Careful Practice Setup

If you are going out to the range to work on one or two things per practice session, then you should consider setting up in an efficient manner. For example, if you are going to work on a practice stage focused on shooting on the move and you plan to shoot a couple of drills on the "Standard Practice Setup," then when you set up the range for the day, you can set that up as part of your practice stage. That way, you won't need to reposition any targets.

This advice can be carried further. If you set up a practice drill or stage, then you always have a target that you can run single-target drills on. For example, it is always an option to shoot a practice stage, and then use one of the targets for "Bill Drills," or perhaps for "The Dots." Structure your practice sessions so you can get multiple things accomplished without needing to reposition anything.

Focus

When you are training, focus up! You need to be mentally engaged, not just going through the motions. You need to pay attention to your points and your time. You need to analyze every performance. You need to constantly be in problem-solving mode.

Now, this doesn't leave a lot of time for other things. You don't want to be fielding phone calls or supervising other shooters. When you are at the range training, be all there.

Don't Be Too Friendly with People

When I am on the range doing training, I try not to get too involved in conversations with people. It seems to me that most shooters spend more time jaw jacking than they do actually shooting. I do feel like a bit of a jerk at the range sometimes, because people are just trying to be friendly. The fact is, friendly people are interfering with your progress as a shooter.

In order to keep people from chatting me up too much, I try to wear hearing protection at all times. Keeping your ears on tends to discourage people from striking up conversation. If someone starts talking, I am nice to them, but I make it real clear that my focus is on shooting.

Choose Training Partners Carefully

If you are going to train with someone else, I recommend you choose that person very carefully. Training with a casual shooter, or someone with wildly disparate goals than yours, can be extremely counterproductive. The time that you should be pushing yourself and learning new things can turn into jaw jacking or just dicking around. Now, don't get me wrong, that stuff is certainly entertaining. However, at some point you need to decide if you are going to be a social shooter (nothing wrong with that), or a competitive shooter.

On the other hand, having a highly motivated and intelligent training partner can push your shooting to the next level. Having someone that can observe you, provide feedback, help keep you on track, and so on is a great thing.

If possible, choose someone with a different skill set than you. If you run around stages and put up fast stage times, then it can be really helpful to pair up with a shooter that is extremely accurate. You can learn that person's skill set and add it to your repertoire.

Consider Your Range Situation

I am a member of five different ranges. Each range is a different distance from my house, has different props available, different bay setups, and different hours of availability. I juggle all those memberships so I can maximize my options when it comes time to train. There is a club available 40 minutes from my house at which I can always work on big field courses. Another club where I can have 10 bays to myself (if I want) is about 90 minutes away. There is a super tiny one-bay club 15 minutes away. The list goes on. In any event, range distance and availability dictates a few things to me.

I make sure I schedule marksmanship training for the closer (but crappier) clubs. I can set up those drills quickly and easily. I schedule more complicated stuff for the ranges where I have more of a drive.

If you are in a similar situation, you need to make similar considerations. It is common for people to have access to an indoor range near their home, but they need to make a long drive to an outdoor range. That means you need to plan your training accordingly if you are going to be bouncing between ranges. Usually indoor ranges are restrictive, so plan to do stuff that will work within the rules for that range. Save the things you can't do indoors for the outdoor range.

Load Up Your Mags

I recommend that you largely ignore magazine capacity restrictions for the purpose of training. For example, if you are a Production or Single Stack shooter, don't restrict yourself to some level of ammunition. It is much more convenient to put a lot of bullets in your magazines. That way, you don't have to stop the party to reload as often. Frequently, students in classes will feel some sort of need to restrict themselves to the division max capacity. Honestly, it will not negatively affect your shooting to fill your mags up.

On the other hand, if you are shooting a high-capacity division, you should feel free to force yourself to reload even when it wouldn't be necessary in a match situation. For example, some of the drills in the movement skills section are excellent places to force yourself to reload. Don't neglect the practice just because you wouldn't have to do it in a match.

You Don't Always Need to Paste

This is dangerous advice to be giving, but in the interest of honesty, I am going to go forward with it. **You don't need to paste the targets after every single string of fire in practice.** Personally, during certain types of practice, I don't paste all that often. It saves a considerable amount of time, and it saves a bit of money for the pasters.

It may seem cryptic for me to say that this advice is dangerous, but understand that one of the key benefits of livefire is that you are able to see where every single round goes. By not pasting, you are going to negate that to a large degree. This can be a problem. You may be firing misses and not know it. You may not be sure which shot went where. So, the advice to not paste every string comes with some stipulations.

If there is a real chance of you shooting a miss on a target, then you absolutely need to restore it between strings. I reserve the "not pasting" advice for targets I am certain that I will hit. For example, training on 25 yard head boxes is tough. I can't be sure I will hit them every shot, so I need to paste them every string to hold myself accountable for where my shots are going. This is largely skill level dependent. **If there is any doubt at all, paste after every string.**

Chapter 12
ODDS AND ENDS

I have this section to include some ideas that need to be discussed, but perhaps didn't cleanly fit into some other part of the book. I realize that there may be a lot of questions raised by earlier portions of this book, and this section will answer them. The stuff in here is extremely important!

What Is a Drill?

One fundamental question that I assume most people know the answer to is, "What is a drill?" If you don't know the answer, then pay attention.

A drill is an exercise. It is a learning tool. You shoot a drill repeatedly, paying attention to whatever elements of your technique that the drill instructs you to pay attention to. Over time, by working through a variety of drills, you should improve.

This is different than a "test." Some instructors advocate shooting certain tests one time, and using that to gauge your skill level. This isn't necessarily a bad idea, but it is different than working through a drill. Remember, a test is something that you take occasionally. A drill is a practice method.

The Mental Game Is Always Happening

You may read through this book and wonder about working on your "mental game." Now, I realize that the concept of mental game may be a bit fuzzy. Not everyone includes the same ideas in how they conceptualize the mental

game. However, the point I want to make is that your mental game training should always be operating. Your mental game needs to be in effect as you work through these drills.

For example, there are lots of concepts that I would consider to be part of my mental game.

I "program" a stage into my mind before I shoot it. I do this by doing detailed visualizations of the way I want to shoot the stage. I have a detailed "make ready" routine where I load my gun and go through one last visualization of the stage. In any event, going through all these ideas in detail would take several chapters. (It actually did take me several chapters in *Practical Pistol*.) The point I want to make here is that you should be practicing your visualization and such on the practice range as you work through drills.

It may seem like it is unnecessary, but remember you are training yourself for the high-pressure environment of major match competition. When you are under pressure, you will find yourself to be prone to making mental errors. If you work your mental game the whole time during practice, that process will become habit and even subconscious.

Shot Calling Is Always Happening

Another concept you didn't see much mention of is "shot calling." Of course, shot calling (knowing where rounds will impact at the moment you fire them) is a desirable and useful skill.

You don't need separate drills to work on shot calling, you should *always* be striving to call your shots. It is as simple as that. You don't need to consciously call shots, but if you are watching your sights closely, you will notice if things don't look right. Then, when you are pasting targets, you will see whether you had errant shots or not. Through constantly going through this process you will develop as a good shot caller.

What I don't think is important is to specifically set up drills to work on shot calling. Shot calling is something that is always operating. I do like to run drills in classes that allow people to demonstrate their (lack of) shot calling ability, but that is more designed to give people a kick in the pants rather than actually develop them as a shooter at that moment.

If you are interested in testing your shot calling, you can work at targets that are far enough away that you can't see the holes in the target from the firing line. In that way, you can mentally call the shot before you walk up and see it. For closer targets, you can shoot at a chewed-up target (with unrestored holes all over it) with a fresh target stapled to the back of it. You can then call your shots before walking up and looking at the target on the back. You then restore the back target and repeat. Essentially, you are just using the chewed-up front target to mask where the hits actually are.

Adapting These Drills for Open Guns

As I pointed out before, these times were developed by me for someone looking to be an M or GM in the iron sight divisions (Limited, Production, Limited 10). The times are *not* appropriate for Open guns. Generally speaking, the further away you get from the targets, the more of an advantage the Open guns will get. At close range, the advantage from Open guns is extremely marginal.

If you are looking for specifics, I recommend the following scheme:

Subtract 0.1 second for every draw and every reload.

Subtract .05 seconds from every target for every 10 yards distance it is from you. So, a 30 yard target should subtract 0.15 from the goal time.

What Is Accuracy?

People normally define accuracy by thinking of how many points they dropped. An "A" zone shot is an accurate shot, and anything else is not accurate. That sort of thinking is perfectly serviceable in a match situation, but in practice you may want to think more in terms of hitting aiming "zones" instead of whether or not you hit the "A" zone. There are some circumstances where you might want to change your aiming method to something that will get you a faster time, but will probably cost you some points in trade. If you restrict your thinking to strictly how many "A"s you shoot, then it will interfere with working out how to get a higher hit factor.

Weather Considerations

One thing that you can take note of during your practice is the effect of various weather conditions on your shooting and mental focus.

During cold or wet conditions, you will likely experience some slower drill times. This is nothing to be concerned with; it is just a fact of life. Cold hands make it hard to manipulate the gun quickly. Cold weather means you are burdened with extra layers of clothing. Wet ground can be hazardous to run across at full speed. Be aware of these things in practice and see what you can do to minimize the effects of unpleasant weather.

Practice Mindset vs. Match Mindset
When you are shooting a match, you certainly must be consistent. You don't want to drop points, take big risks, or lose control. The people that are in the running to win a major championship time and time again tend to be consistent and disciplined. Think of that style of shooting as your "match mindset."

In practice, it is permissible to make mistakes. More than that, it is sometimes a requirement to push yourself to the point of failure, or to experiment with new techniques. Without giving yourself "permission to fail" during your practice, you will have a hard time making gains in your skill level after a while.

The point here is that you need to be in control of your mindset at all times. Either you are keeping things tight and disciplined, or you are pushing your limits. If you aren't consciously aware of what mindset you are exercising, you may find yourself cutting loose in a match and being way out of control. You may find yourself doing the same thing over and over again during your practice, unable to make a change that may be helpful.

Breaking the Plateau
You may have gotten this book because you have arrived at a plateau in your skill level. After people are in the sport for a while, the improvement slows down. After you can reload efficiently, draw quickly, shoot decent points, and navigate stages effectively, then improvement will really slow down. How many guys do you know in this situation? They get to A class, then stall out for a couple years. They finish at 85 percent at their area match one year, but then they finish in the same place year after year, never really improving. This is called hitting a plateau, and it happens to everyone eventually.

The first bit of advice I can give is the most important. You can't give up. I personally went through a two-year phase where I didn't make much headway at all in the match results. Reading it on this page, it may not sound like much, but give it some careful consideration. *Two years*. Two years of working through the ideas in this book. Two years of intense training. No measurable difference in the match results during this time. It takes a good bit of mental toughness to work through this without quitting. So many shooters get to the plateau and then quit. I have seen it more times than I can count.

You need to realize that in a sport like USPSA, one of the best assets you can have is persistence. You need to be willing to go out to the range time and time again. You need to be willing to dryfire every day. You need to be willing to try as hard as you can, *and still fail*. If you can't handle a setback or two, you are going to have a hard time climbing your way to the top of USPSA.

One common situation when someone has hit the plateau is that they may need to start paying attention to the details of the sport. Eventually, simply going faster and trying to hit everything may well not be getting it done for you. I have encountered many students in this situation. They may be pretty good in a match situation, but if you carefully dissect their game they could make small improvements to a plethora of skills. Yes, it would take a lot of work to make it happen. That is the point.

As an example, consider the "Standard Practice Setup" in the standard exercises section. Many high-level shooters (Master or Grand Master) are not able to make the goal times for even half of the drills I have listed. That means that if those shooters want to get to an even a higher level of shooting, they need to get to work figuring out how to make things happen for some of the individual drills in that section. Maybe they need to change their technique. Maybe they need to figure out how to efficiently handle targets at some particular distance. Whatever

the issue is, it may take some effort to solve. Systematically working through those problems and figuring things out will take that shooter to the next level.

If you feel your weakness is one specific area of your shooting, and you spend a couple months working on that thing, then you will likely hit a plateau. Don't worry about it. I have often set an aggressive goal and then worked to nail it, only to fail to hit that goal. Let's say, for example, I really want to hit a personal best "Bill Drill" time of 1.50 seconds. I may work at it hard for a few weeks. I may emphasize drawing drills and high-speed shooting drills to try and hit that time. I may well not hit 1.50 seconds. Maybe my best was 1.53 seconds.

Eventually, you will hit a point of diminishing returns. Chasing your short-term goal is more like beating your head against the wall. It helps to move on to some other things, set a different goal, and then come back to whatever you were doing later. When you come back, you will be re-energized and re-invigorated. **Don't get to the point of being demoralized.**

Sometimes, it may be beneficial to focus on a different set of drills for a while if you feel stuck where you are. If you are drilling hard in the standard exercises section, and you aren't getting anywhere, take a break from it. Go do some stage work for a bit; don't keep beating your head against the wall in a section that isn't helping you. Find the next thing and chase it down. When you come back to what you were working on before, you will probably feel refreshed and ready.

Time to Get to the Range

It is my sincere hope that this book has given you a new direction in your training. If not that, then at least some new ideas. I want you to set aggressive goals, get out to the range, and make it happen.

No matter what level of shooter you are, you can get better. No matter whether you are totally hopeless or world class. **You can get better.**

No matter what issues come up during your training, don't give up. Remember, it may take dozens or even hundreds of hours of dedicated training to make a breakthrough, but when the breakthrough happens, it can be a game changer.

GLOSSARY

"A": The maximum point-scoring zone on a USPSA target

Dryfire: Practicing with an unloaded firearm

Googlefu: The ability to use Google with zen-like prowess

Grandbagging: Attempting to obtain a classification that is above your "true" skill level

Group shooting: Shooting a few shots in the same place on the target

Hosefest: Stages that do not have demanding marksmanship challenges

IDPA: International Defensive Pistol Association

Index: Ability to look at a spot and have the sights show up in alignment on that spot

Limited Division: USPSA division defined primarily by allowing everything except optics and compensators

Livefire: Actually firing a gun

Open Division: USPSA division allowing for significant modifications to the competition firearm including optical sights.

Production Division: USPSA division using predominately unmodified firearms

Sandbagging: Attempting to remain in a classification that is below your "true" skill level

Sight focus: Having your optical focus on your sights

Splits: The time between shots

String: A number of shots at a target or group of targets

Strong hand: Your dominant hand

Super squad: The group of the top shooters at USPSA Nationals

Target focus: Having your optical focus on the target you are engaging

Transitions: Moving the gun from one target to another

Trigger freeze: Attempting to pull the trigger so fast that you don't pull it far enough to discharge the gun

Walkthrough: The stage inspection period at a match

Weak hand: Nondominant hand

USPSA: United States Practical Shooting Association

ACKNOWLEDGMENTS

Special Thanks:
I would like to thank guys like Brian Enos, Saul Kirsch, Mike Plaxco, and Rob Leatham. Each of them, and many more, have contributed in some way to this book and my development as a shooter, and they deserve credit.

Editing:
Ronnie Casper once again edited the book. The book would not be possible without him.

Illustrations:
Ronnie Casper contributed all of the diagrams.

Photography:
Lisa Martin, Steph Berry, Sight Picture Media, and Hwansik Kim provided photos.

OTHER TITLES WITH
SKYHORSE PUBLISHING

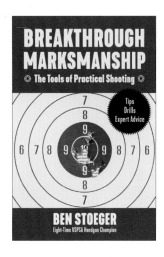

Breakthrough Marksmanship
Ben Stoeger
120 Pages
ISBN: 978-1-5107-7936-5
Price: $15.99

Practical Pistol
Ben Stoeger
216 Pages
ISBN: 978-1-5107-7948-8
Price: $24.99

Practical Shooting Training
Ben Stoeger, Joel Park
336 Pages
ISBN: 978-1-5107-7934-1
Price: $29.99

Adaptive Rifle
Ben Stoeger, Joel Park
144 Pages
ISBN: 978-1-5107-7946-4
Price: $24.99